#1 INTERNATIONAL BEST SELLER

FREE THINKER

The Art of Becoming Who You Are Meant to Be

The 7 Principles To Living Authentically

James Rolevski

FREE THINKER

The Art of Becoming Who You Are Meant to Be

The 7 Principles To Living Authentically

Free Thinker: The Art of Becoming Who You Are Meant To Be

1st Edition. 2026 v1.5

ASIN: 978-1-923223-70-7 (Amazon Kindle)

ISBN: 978-1-923223-71-4 (Amazon) PAPERBACK

ISBN: 978-1-923223-73-8 (Amazon) HARDCOVER

ISBN: 978-1-923223-72-1 (Ingram Spark) PAPERBACK

ISBN: 978-1-923223-74-5 (Ingram Spark) HARDCOVER

ISBN: 978-1-923223-70-7 (D2D)

CONTACT THE AUTHOR:

Website: www.jamesrolevski.com

Font Type:

(Header) Avenir Black

(Content) Minion Pro

Table of Contents

About The Author

James Rolevski is a life coach, speaker and author who teaches people how to think independently in a world built on influence.

After growing up in a rough environment marked by loss, addiction, and mental illness, he spent years reading obsessively and rebuilding himself from the ground up. That raw experience became the foundation for his work in self-development, which he gained not from theory but from life.

Free Thinker cuts through the noise to help readers develop genuine self-mastery. James writes from an introspective lens that doesn't tell people what to think but shows them how.

James' goal is straightforward: to help individuals find truth through their own understanding, rather than relying on someone else's blueprint.

Dedication

To Julie, Anthony, Emily, Jacob and Vanessa.

Vesna Rolevski (1970–2001) The Brightest Star in the Sky

The 7 Principles of Free Thinking

Claim Your Beliefs

Curiosity Without Fear

Pursue the Unconventional Path

7 Principles of Free Thinking

Listen Deeper, Speak Smarter

Write Your Own Script

Question Authority

Challenge Cultural Norms

The Awakening Moment

The Awakening Moment

"The privilege of a lifetime is to become who you truly are."

— Carl Jung

The moments that change your life never arrive with applause. They slip in quietly, disguised as the kind of night you've lived a hundred times — until suddenly you realize you can't keep living this way.

Mine came on a rain-soaked evening when everything felt heavy: the pills, the drinking, the expectations, the noise inside my own head. I'd spent years trying to fix myself with distractions, routines, labels, and whatever advice was loudest at the time. None of it worked. None of it touched the real problem — I wasn't thinking for myself. I was performing a life I didn't believe in.

That night, something inside me finally cracked.

I walked outside into the storm, barefoot, as if instinct was dragging me there. The rain hit hard and cold, but it was the first thing in years that felt honest. I stood there, soaked, letting every mistake, every inherited belief, every expectation wash off me. It felt like someone had lifted a curtain. The world didn't change — but I did.

A simple thought rose, clear and sharp:

"You're allowed to start again."

Not in a dramatic, movie-like way. More like a truth I'd been avoiding because it required me to actually show up for myself. That was the moment I understood something most people never stop to question: you can live decades without ever making a single decision that's truly yours.

We inherit beliefs without realizing it.

We follow scripts we didn't write.

We wear identities that don't fit

And one day, we wake up wondering why nothing feels right.

The awakening isn't about perfection or enlightenment. It's not a spiritual explosion or some grand revelation. It's quieter than that. It's the moment you stop running from your own truth. The moment you finally admit that the life you're living isn't the one you want. The moment you hear your own voice for the first time in years — and trust it.

That night in the rain, I forgave people who never apologized. I forgave myself for everything I'd done and everything I'd avoided. And with that forgiveness came a strange calm, the kind that tells you the next chapter of your life won't look like the last.

The awakening moment is simple:

You realize the biggest betrayal isn't disappointing other people — it's abandoning yourself.

From that point on, everything shifts. Not instantly, but inevitably. You start questioning instead of accepting. You listen instead of obeying. You stop outsourcing your decisions to the loudest voice in the room. And slowly, you become someone you actually recognize.

Your own awakening might look different — a conversation, a breakdown, a quiet morning when something inside you finally says, "enough." But when it comes, you'll feel it. And when you do, there's no returning to autopilot.

This book begins at that point — the moment you wake up, step out of the storm, and finally take ownership of your life.

Your turn starts now.

Why and How

Why I Wrote This Book

Let's begin with my life — not because it's more important than yours, but because you deserve to know where these words come from. I'll only share the turning points, the moments that shaped the free thinker I eventually became. The rest of this book is about you — your awakening; your moment of clarity. But before you get there, I want you to see how I found mine.

My story began in pain. I was five years old when my mother passed away suddenly. At that age, you can feel sadness, but you can't make sense of it. One day, she was there — warm, loving, everything familiar — and then she was gone. I didn't understand death. I just knew that life had shifted forever. I developed a neurological disorder called Tourette's syndrome.

Six months later, my father met another woman, and a year after my mother's death, we moved in with her and her three children. He was unstable, emotionally and financially, and carried a gambling addiction that swallowed everything — our property, our inheritance, our security. I learned early that the spinning lights of a poker machine could devour an entire life. That's why gambling never once tempted me.

My father married his new partner, and on the surface, we looked like one big happy family. But behind closed doors, none of us — not me, my siblings, or my stepbrothers — were fooled. The only real comfort we had came from my auntie, who became our protector and guiding light. She was the one person I could count on to remind me that things would one day be okay.

Four years later, my father divorced his second wife. I was ten. It was a relief to everyone involved. But the damage was already done. I was entering my teenage years carrying a storm inside me that I didn't yet know how to name.

By fourteen, that storm turned into rebellion. I grew up rough. My friends and I spent our early teens drinking liquor and smoking marijuana, convincing ourselves we were men when we were just lost boys trying to numb our pain. Trouble seemed to follow us everywhere. Fights, parties, chaos. We were surrounded by darkness and thought it was normal. That's how far removed we were from anything resembling a healthy upbringing.

When the teenage parties faded, the drugs and alcohol remained. After school, I entered adulthood already damaged — and it showed. A bad breakup, my father's rehab visits, and my own mental decline led me into the waiting arms of the medical system. Within a short time, I was on three different prescription pills, each one designed to dull the symptoms of depression, anxiety, schizophrenia, and bipolar disorder. None of them healed me. They only numbed me.

Those pills, combined with six years of heavy drinking, nearly erased who I was. Alcohol became my medicine, my friend, and my prison. My twenties were a blur of ambition and destruction. I was working long hours, chasing the dream of becoming a multimillionaire, but underneath it all, I was exhausted, directionless, and completely disconnected from myself.

Eventually, I cracked. The weight of it all became unbearable. I went back to the doctor, desperate for answers, and instead was given stronger doses and new labels. My mental health worsened. I gained weight. My confidence vanished. My nights were spent drinking alone, my days trying to function through fog and fatigue.

Then one day, I'd had enough. Something inside me whispered, Stop. I went back to my doctor and told him I wanted off the medication. Slowly, painfully, I began to wean myself off two of the strongest pills. The withdrawals were brutal — insomnia, cold sweats, vomiting, total exhaustion. I still worked part-time through it, somehow surviving those two months of mental and physical torment. I dropped twenty kilos and, for the first time in years, looked alive again.

When I finally came through the other side, it was as if a curtain had lifted. I could feel again. I could think again. I could see who I'd become — and who I no longer wanted to be.

Sobriety gave me confidence, and confidence gave me ego. I started dating again, feeling attractive, sharp, powerful — too powerful. My ego became its own addiction, and looking back, I can laugh at how inflated it was. I met a woman who made me realize that. Our connection was innocent, genuine, a spark I hadn't felt for years. It didn't last, but it opened something in me. This marked the beginning of my real transformation.

That short-lived romance pushed me into solitude — and solitude became my salvation. I decided to heal, to rebuild myself from the ground up. Without pills, without alcohol, without distraction. The first thing I rebuilt was my body. I started training six days a week, running ten kilometers every morning, eating clean, studying nutrition, and gut health. Every sweat-soaked session became therapy.

I entered what I called monk mode. No drinking, no partying, no dating. Just discipline, prayer, reflection, and work. I filled my days with weightlifting, journaling, and nightly gratitude. I studied self-development obsessively, read the Bible, and practiced stillness. For the first time, I was alone with my own thoughts — and it terrified me.

But slowly, solitude turned into strength. I started forming opinions of my own. I realized how much of my life had been borrowed from other people's beliefs. I learned to trust my own reasoning, my intuition, and my moral compass.

When I exited monk mode, I felt calm and reborn — and ready for love again. I went on a date with a woman I'd spoken to throughout that period. We clicked immediately. Within a month, we were together, and for a while, life was beautiful.

Then came another test. My father, with whom I was still living, began resenting my progress. He became furious, and one night it got aggressive. I left, moving in temporarily with my auntie — the same woman who had protected me all those years ago. My spirit was shaken, but I was determined not to lose myself again.

Living there was necessary. This was a time when I was under a massive amount of stress. I couldn't sleep. I lost my rhythm and my solitude. I leaned on my girlfriend for comfort, but the old chaos was creeping back. I was reading, studying, and trying to hold my mind together while my body and heart were exhausted. I had found clarity once, and now I had to fight to keep it.

In the middle of all that struggle, I turned to faith. I started praying daily, and for the first time, I felt a connection to something higher than myself. God began testing me through suffering, but this time I didn't break — I surrendered. That surrender became the most profound experience of my life. I awakened spiritually. I felt peace. For a few days, the world looked different — lighter, clearer, realer.

But growth never happens in straight lines. My relationship began to drift apart under the weight of everything I was processing. It was over. I moved into my new place alone, carrying heartbreak, exhaustion, and a strange new serenity. I missed her deeply, but I refused to let pain harden my heart again. She had been my light in a dark time — the human reminder that love is possible even when life feels unbearable. I still carry gratitude for her, always will.

A few days after the breakup, I went to a public event with friends. The crowd was wild — drunken chaos all around — yet I stood still, calm, unshaken. I felt something I'd never felt before: total peace. The kind that can't be bought or explained.

When I got home that night, it was raining. I stood outside for hours in the downpour, listening to music, letting the water wash everything away — the pain, the guilt, the weight of three decades. In that moment, I forgave everyone who'd hurt me. I forgave myself most of all.

Life had to destroy me completely so that I could rebuild. That night, I let go of everything that wasn't mine — all the opinions, judgments, mistakes, and masks I'd been wearing.

That was the true awakening. The moment I became a free thinker.

My entire journey — from the loss of my mother to the addiction, the pills, the heartbreaks, and the solitude — was all leading here. Every moment of suffering became a lesson. Every mistake became material for growth. Every tear watered the seed of clarity that eventually bloomed into wisdom.

It was brutal, beautiful, and absolutely necessary.

Because through all of it, I found the one thing that matters most — the strength to think for myself, and the courage to live from truth.

And that's why I wrote this book. To pass that clarity on to you — so you can find your own moment of awakening, your own reason to rise, and your own path to freedom.

How to Use This Book

This book isn't meant to be read from start to finish unless you want to. Think of it more like a toolkit; something you dip into whenever you need clarity, a challenge, or a reminder of who you're trying to become.

Here's the simplest way to use it:

1. Start with any of the principles. Each principle stands on its own. If you're struggling with confidence, jump to the chapters on self-belief. If you're feeling stuck, read the sections on questioning your assumptions. If you're rebuilding your life, solitude and reflection are the best places to start.

2. Treat the principles like lenses. Every chapter shows you a different way of thinking — critical, intuitive, practical, reflective. Try them on. Some will feel natural. Others will stretch you.

3. Come back to the book often. Your thinking evolves as your life does. The chapter that doesn't land today might be the one that changes everything six months from now.

4. Use the book actively, not passively. Pause when something hits you. Write. Question. Apply. The point isn't to memorize ideas but to use them.

5. Build your own path. Free Thinker is not a rulebook. It's a guide for discovering how you think. The goal is not to transform you into someone who thinks like me. Take what fits, leave what doesn't, and shape the rest into something that's yours.

There's no time limit. No particular order. No set requirement to finish the book.

Your job is to read with awareness.

Your goal is to free your mind.

Part I

The Wake-Up Call

Great Thinkers and How They Changed the World

Throughout history, certain thinkers have stood apart—not merely for their intelligence, but for their willingness to question authority, challenge cultural norms, and pursue unconventional paths. These individuals shared common traits: courage, strong will, fearlessness, and relentless perseverance in seeking the truth. Although often misunderstood by their contemporaries, their independent thinking changed the world.

Look at anyone history remembers. They didn't ask permission to think differently.

They studied the rules, understood why they existed, then decided which ones to keep and which ones to rewrite. They didn't change the entire world—they changed their corner of it. A city. A field. An industry. A family. That was enough.

You don't need to be famous. You just need to be honest. The people who walk through life with that spark? They're not smarter. They're just willing to think for themselves and deal with the consequences.

The following eight figures exemplify different types of thinking. Each excelled in their particular mode of thought, demonstrating what becomes possible when we think freely. They were human, like us, which means their achievements are not beyond our reach.

They were all great thinkers in their own way. We all use different types of thinking in our lives to achieve our goals. These are examples of how these free thinkers excelled in the 8 types of thinking I have written about in this book.

All 8 historical and cultural figures stood out in their societies—you might not know them, but if you see them walking around, you can tell from the aura they have that they are on another level of human experience. This is the level we all dream of being at.

Who says we can't be?

They are humans like me and you, so who says we can't be extraordinary free thinkers like them? These aren't just words of encouragement; it really is possible for anyone to become a free thinker if they believe themselves capable.

Now, let's take a brief look into the minds of some of the most influential thinkers in history. I chose these amazing thinkers because they have been inspirations for me, showing me how one individual can live an extraordinary life, which is the biggest blessing we can receive.

Rosa Parks – Independent Thinker

Rosa Parks became an icon of the civil rights movement through a single act of moral courage. Born in Tuskegee, Alabama, on 4 February 1913, Parks refused to give up her bus seat to a white person on 1 December 1955 just because she was an African-American during the Jim Crow era. She was arrested for her defiance, sparking nationwide attention and leading to the Montgomery bus boycott.

Parks' quiet but firm refusal exemplified independent thinking. She followed her own beliefs about justice rather than conforming to unjust social norms. She thought for herself, taking great personal risk by refusing to give in to unjust laws that oppressed the African American people.

Beyond that pivotal moment, and throughout her long and extraordinary life, Parks achieved many other notable accomplishments. She remained active in the civil rights movement and later founded the Rosa and Raymond Parks Institute for Self Development, a nonprofit dedicated to youth empowerment and civil rights education.

Her words capture the essence of independent thought: "I was just tired of giving in" and "You must never be fearful about what you are doing when it is right."

Rosa Parks' legacy lives on and has inspired generations to stand against injustice.

Steve Jobs – Intuitive Thinker

Born 24 February 1955, in San Francisco, Steve Jobs revolutionized technology through his intuitive vision. After dropping out of college, he traveled to India to study Zen Buddhism, seeking enlightenment and the spiritual understanding that would later inform his creative approach. He also consumed psychedelics to expand his mind.

His intuition created an empire that changed how the world works today. He is an entrepreneur and inventor known for co-founding Apple.

Steve Jobs used his intuitive thinking to achieve many notable results. He consistently prioritized his gut feeling over conventional market research. When developing the iPhone, research indicated consumers preferred physical keyboards. Jobs ignored this data, choosing a touchscreen design instead. His intuition proved correct—the iPhone transformed the mobile industry.

Steve showed us the power of "following our hearts." This positive attitude, which he used to project his beliefs onto the world with the invention of his products, brought me to the realization that intuition and hope can change a person and the world itself.

Through Apple, Jobs pioneered the personal computer revolution and created products that became dominant in their fields: the Macintosh, iPhone, iPad, and MacBook. His philosophy, captured in the phrase "Stay hungry, stay foolish," demonstrated how intuitive thinking can reshape entire industries.

Steve Jobs died on 5 October 2011 at 56 years of age.

Marcus Aurelius – Reflective Thinker

Marcus Aurelius, Roman Emperor and Stoic philosopher (121–180 AD), exemplified reflective thinking through his commitment to self-examination and philosophical inquiry. His private journal, Meditations, remains one of history's most profound works of introspection. He has deeply shaped my own reflective thinking.

In *Meditations*, Marcus Aurelius documented his daily reflections on conduct, Stoic principles, and self-improvement. The work reveals his use of solitude and writing to deepen his understanding of life, duty, and virtue.

This book was a game-changer for me. I resonated deeply with his thoughts on life and used that knowledge to deepen my sense of self and achieve greater self-improvement each day, especially through nightly self-reflection.

We all need solitude so we can step back and enjoy a moment of silence to gain clarity after navigating the chaos of the external world.

Marcus Aurelius' quotes are incredibly inspiring and encouraging. His insights continue to resonate several millennia later: "You have power over your mind, not outside events. Realize this and you will find strength," and "Dwell on the beauty of life, watch the stars, and see yourself running with them."

Through reflective thinking, Marcus Aurelius demonstrated how inner examination strengthens character and wisdom.

Marcus Aurelius was a wise man who spread Stoic philosophy and inspired generations to seek inner strength.

Angela Duckworth – Practical Thinker

Angela Duckworth, born on 26 October 1970 in the United States, demonstrates practical thinking through her focus on applying ideas in real-world settings. Rather than letting her ideas die as theory, she consistently tested them where outcomes could be observed and measured. Her work shows that thinking only matters when it leads to action and results.

Before becoming a psychologist, Duckworth worked as a management consultant and later as a school teacher. These experiences exposed her to human struggle and effort in everyday environments, leading her to question why some people persist while others give up, even when talent appears equal. Instead of accepting common assumptions, she sought practical explanations grounded in evidence.

Her research led to the concept of grit — perseverance and sustained effort toward long-term goals. Duckworth approached this idea practically by measuring it, testing it across different environments, and refining it based on real outcomes. She showed that success is not just about intelligence or motivation, but about consistent effort over time.

As a professor of psychology and founder of Character Lab, Duckworth continues to apply thinking to reality rather than abstraction. Her work reflects a practical mindset: question assumptions, test ideas, and improve through feedback. This approach demonstrates how clear, disciplined thinking leads to meaningful progress.

Pablo Picasso – Creative Thinker

Pablo Picasso (1881–1973) was one of the twentieth century's most influential artists. He was born in Spain, and died in France at the age of 91.

His creative thinking stemmed from being bold, fiercely original, and fearlessly experimenting across a range of media, including painting, sculpture, and ceramics. He was an inventive nonconformist.

Picasso's genius lay in his constant reinvention and ability to perceive the world differently from others. His creative thinking has led to the production of some of the most famous artworks in history. He developed Cubism, depicting subjects from various viewpoints simultaneously using abstract, geometric forms. His masterpieces include Les Demoiselles d'Avignon and Guernica.

Instead of remaining one-dimensional, Picasso mixed up his style to create new feelings and emotions, using reinvention to expand his mindset, and express his true self. Pablo Picasso exemplified this through his art, consistently producing great work.

His words illuminate creative thinking: "Every act of creation is first an act of destruction," and "The purpose of art is washing the dust of daily life off our souls."

Picasso challenged conventional artistic norms, permanently altering how we understand and create art.

Aristotle – Logical Thinker

This logical thinker has shaped my thoughts and has been a major influence on cultivating logical thinking to be my strongest type of free thinking. Aristotle was an ancient Greek philosopher born in 384 BCE in Stayira and historians believe he died in Châlus in 322 BCE, either at 61 or 62. Educated under Plato, Aristotle developed his free thinking and logic through empirical observation, studying nature directly to derive reasoned conclusions.

His work in biology exemplifies this approach. By observing how octopuses use their tentacles to catch prey, he applied logical reasoning to understand their function and purpose.

Aristotle's achievements are numerous. He founded formal logic, the study of reasoning based on structure rather than content. His works, including The Organon and Nicomachean Ethics, laid the foundations for Western philosophy and empirical science.

His insights endure:

- "All men by nature desire to know."
- "We are what we repeatedly do. Excellence, then, is not an act, but a habit."
- "It is the mark of an educated mind to be able to entertain a thought without accepting it."

People consider him the Father of Logic, the founder of biology and zoology, and a pioneer of virtue ethics. Aristotle is one of the greatest logical thinkers.

Michael Shermer – Skeptical Thinker

Michael Shermer, American science writer and executive director of the Skeptics Society, represents modern skeptical thinking. He advocates for evidence-based reasoning and critical examination of claims. He goes against cultural norms.

Shermer demands evidence proportional to claims, particularly when debunking pseudoscience, like UFO conspiracies or paranormal phenomena. He distinguishes between skepticism (open-minded inquiry) and cynicism (closed-minded rejection), remaining willing to accept claims supported by sufficient evidence.

In 1992, he founded the Skeptic magazine, promoting scientific skepticism, critical thinking, and rationality, while dismantling conspiracy theories and pseudoscience. The publication has gained recognition in academic and scientific communities.

His perspectives include: "I'm not a skeptic to debunk; I want to know what's true," and "Smart people believe weird things because they are skilled at defending beliefs they arrived at for non-smart reasons."

In an age of misinformation, Shermer's work empowers independent thinking.

Socrates - Critical Thinker

The ancient Greek philosopher, Socrates, had a brilliant mind. He was born in Athens, Greece, in 470 BCE and died there in 399 BCE.

Socrates has shaped me in such an impactful way, especially during business meetings, for example, where people explain a problem to me and I use my critical thinking skills to ask questions and encourage them to elaborate on their reasoning.

Exemplifying critical thinking through systematic questioning, his Socratic Method involves asking probing questions to clarify thoughts, expose contradictions, and arrive at deeper truths. This technique remains powerful in modern contexts—from business meetings to personal reflection—helping people examine their reasoning and discover underlying principles.

Critical thinking is fundamental for free thinkers in the pursuit of knowledge and truth. I use the Socratic Method in my business meetings. I ask questions for clarification so I can better understand the essence of the conversation and find the best solution available.

Critical thinking is key for free thinkers to acquire knowledge.

Socrates is considered the founder of Western philosophy. Though he left no writings, his student, Plato, recorded his dialogs, preserving his ideas for posterity. Plato was famous in his own right, and his writings made Socrates one of the most important figures in philosophy.

The following famous quotes from Socrates capture the essence of critical thinking:

- "I know that I am intelligent because I know that I know nothing."
- "To find yourself, think for yourself."
- "The unexamined life is not worth living."

Socrates changed the world by revolutionizing philosophy and transforming how humans think about knowledge, ethics, and existence.

In summary, these eight individuals demonstrate that excellence in thinking takes many forms. Each mastered their particular mode while sharing fundamental traits: courage, independence, and commitment to truth. As we explore the eight types of thinking in the following chapters, we'll discover how to develop these same qualities in ourselves.

Introduction

"Most people would sooner die than think; in fact, they do so."

— Bertrand Russell

Tomorrow morning, find a crowded place. A train station, a coffee shop, or a sidewalk during lunch hour. Just watch.

Notice how everyone looks busy. Everyone looks normal. They're dressed, moving with purpose, checking phones, carrying bags. But scan the crowd carefully. How many people actually look awake? Not caffeinated—awake. How many move like they know exactly why they're here?

You'll count maybe two or three out of a hundred.

The rest? They're fine. Functional. But there's no spark behind their eyes. They've learned the pattern—school, job, family, retirement—and they're walking it out. Technically, nothing's wrong. But nothing's particularly right either.

The few who stand out aren't louder or better dressed. They just occupy space differently. They made decisions you can't see, and those decisions show. They're not performing with confidence. They're not trying to impress anyone. There's just something solid about them, like they know something the rest of the crowd hasn't figured out yet.

What they know is simple: they decided to think for themselves.

Time to check in ...

Thinking for yourself sounds obvious until you realize how rare it actually is. Check in with yourself. Like most people, you're probably outsourcing your thinking to whoever's loudest—parents, bosses, influencers, whatever's trending. You adopt beliefs without testing them. You follow paths because those paths exist, not because they lead anywhere worth going.

And then you wonder why life feels hollow.

You already know what matters to you. Career, family, creativity, health, spirituality—whatever it is, it's already there. The problem isn't a lack of knowledge. It's noise. You've been handed a script: get the degree, climb the ladder, buy the house, repeat. That script works for some people. Maybe not you.

Purpose doesn't come from following someone else's blueprint. It comes from sitting with yourself long enough to hear what you actually want, then building toward that. Maybe you've skipped this part. You've hit 40 and realized you've been living someone else's life. Most people do this.

You got the job your parents approved of. You stayed in a relationship because breaking up seemed harder than staying. You built a life that looks good on paper but feels empty in practice.

Introspection is uncomfortable. It forces you to confront the gap between who you are and who you're pretending to be. It asks questions you might not want to answer. It reveals that some of the beliefs you've been carrying around aren't even yours—you just picked them up somewhere along the way and never bothered to examine them.

That discomfort is the price of clarity. You can avoid it and spend your life on autopilot, or you can sit with it and find out what you're actually built for. There's no middle ground. You either think for yourself or you let someone else do it for you.

But when someone else does your thinking, you end up living their life, not yours.

There's no single "right" way to think

Some people are intuitive: they read the room, trust their gut, and see patterns before they're obvious. Others are practical: they test, adjust, measure, and refine. Some are creative, some are skeptical, and some are logical.

You'll have a natural lean. Maybe you're the person who questions everything until it makes sense. Maybe you're the one who sees the vision first and figures out the details later. Both ways work, but you have to know which person you are, because success comes from using your strengths, not mimicking someone else's.

An entrepreneur who thinks creatively will build differently from one who thinks systematically. The creative one might launch fast, iterate wildly, and chase inspiration wherever it leads. The systematic one might plan meticulously, test every assumption, and scale methodically. Both can succeed. Both can fail. The difference isn't the method—it's whether the method matches the person using it.

A trainer who thinks practically will focus on measurable results. Sets, reps, body composition, performance metrics. A trainer who thinks intuitively might read clients differently, adjust on feel, notice patterns that data doesn't capture. Neither approach is superior. But if the practical thinker tries to operate on intuition alone, they'll second-guess everything. And if the intuitive thinker forces themselves into rigid systems, they'll lose the edge that makes them effective.

This is why copying someone else rarely works. If you see someone successful, you might try to reverse-engineer their process only to find it doesn't work for you. Their process works for them because it fits how they think. When you tried to force it onto yourself, it felt awkward and exhausting. You were wearing someone else's clothes.

The goal isn't to adopt someone else's thinking style. It's to figure out yours, then refine it until it's sharp.

But how do you do this?

Experimentation. You'll fail. You'll try approaches that don't fit. You'll realize you've been doing something the hard way because you were too stubborn to admit it wasn't working. That's fine. Failure teaches you what success can't: where your edges are, what breaks under pressure, what you need to stop doing.

Chances are, like most people, you've avoided this process. You've found one method that sort of works and ridden it forever, even when it stopped producing results. You were afraid that if you questioned your approach, you'd have to admit you were wrong. So you've kept doing the same thing, wondering why nothing has changed.

Thinking for yourself means being willing to be wrong. It means testing your assumptions, noticing when something isn't working, and changing course. It means staying flexible while everyone around you insists there's only one way to do things.

Here's the part no one warns you about: the people closest to you might not support this. Parents who want stability. Friends who feel threatened by your changes. Partners who liked the version of you that didn't ask questions.

This isn't about rebellion. It's about responsibility. You're the one who has to live your life. Not them. If you spend fifty years building someone else's dream to avoid disappointing them, that's on you.

The cost of thinking for yourself is discomfort. The cost of not thinking for yourself is a lifetime of dissatisfaction you can't name.

When you start making decisions based on what you actually believe instead of what you think you're supposed to believe, people notice. And some of them won't like it. They'll call you selfish. They'll say you've changed, and not in a good way. They'll remind you of all the reasons you should stay where you are.

Sometimes they're trying to protect you. Sometimes they're trying to protect themselves. When you change, it forces them to confront their own choices. If you're willing to take risks, and they're not, your existence becomes a mirror. It's easier to convince you to stop than to examine why they haven't started.

You'll lose people over this. Not everyone, but some. It will hurt, but the alternative is worse. You'll spend decades making yourself smaller so that other people feel comfortable. You'll look back at the age 70 and realize you never actually lived. Instead, you just managed other people's expectations until you ran out of time.

At 70, you'll realize you're the same person you were at 18, just older. Same fears, same excuses, same autopilot. That's not a life. That's a long, slow fade.

But, what can we do about it?

The thing is, as with most people, you'll probably accept this without a fight. You'll tell yourself you're being realistic, responsible, and mature. You'll convince yourself that wanting more is naive or greedy. You'll watch other people take risks and tell yourself they just got lucky.

Luck has less to do with it than you think. People who build lives they're proud of aren't lucky—they're intentional. If you do this, you'll decide what matters, ignore what doesn't, and keep moving. You'll also fail constantly. Get rejected. And have moments where you question everything.

But you won't stop thinking for yourself. You won't hand the reins back to someone else just because the path got hard.

You can do this. You don't need permission. You don't need a perfect plan. You just need to start paying attention to what you actually think instead of what you've been told to think.

How to start

Go somewhere public tomorrow. Count how many people seem fully present versus those who are moving on autopilot. Write the number down. This isn't judgment—it's calibration. You're learning to see the difference between people who are living and people who are just getting through the day.

Answer one question honestly: If you could design the next five years of your life, ignoring all outside expectations—money, approval, tradition—what would you actually build? Write it down. Don't edit. Don't make it reasonable. Just write what's true.

You'll probably hesitate. You'll think of all the reasons it's not practical. You'll hear voices in your head explaining why it can't work. Write it anyway. Those voices aren't facts—they're fears dressed up as logic.

Finally, identify one inherited belief. Pick something you believe about how life "should" work. Where did that belief come from? Your parents? School? Your culture? Now ask: Do I actually agree with this, or did I just never question it?

Maybe you believe you need a stable job to be successful. Where did that come from? Maybe it's true for you. Maybe it's not. You won't know until you examine it.

Maybe you believe asking for help is weak. Who taught you that? Is it serving you, or is it just making everything harder than it needs to be?

Maybe you believe you're supposed to have everything figured out by 30. Says who? And what happens if you don't? Does your life end, or do you just keep going?

You don't have to change these beliefs. Just notice them. See where they came from. Decide if they're yours or if you're just carrying them because no one ever told you that you could put them down.

Thinking for yourself isn't rebellion. It's a responsibility.

Right now ...

This week, make one decision based solely on what you believe is right, not what someone else expects. Start small: how you spend your evening, what you say no to, what you prioritize. See what happens. Notice how it feels.

It might feel uncomfortable at first. You might feel guilty. You might worry you're being selfish or difficult. That's normal. You've spent years training yourself to prioritize other people's opinions over your own. It takes time to reverse that.

But pay attention to what happens after the discomfort fades. Notice if you feel more solid, more certain, more like yourself. Notice if the decision you made actually hurt anyone, or if you were just afraid it would. Notice if the people who matter still respect you, or if the only ones upset were the ones who benefited from you not thinking for yourself.

This is how it starts. One decision. Then another. Then another. And eventually, you realize you're not following a script anymore. You're writing your own.

The rest of this book will show you the seven ways of thinking that define a true free thinker; the seven keys to unlocking freedom, creativity, and clarity. You'll learn to see the patterns beneath illusion, question what's accepted, and understand yourself in ways you never have before.

Now it's time.

No more autopilot.

No more borrowed beliefs.

It's time to think.

Part II

The Principles of Free Thinking

What are the Seven Principles?

The seven principles of Free Thinking are:

1. Claim Your Beliefs
2. Curiosity Without Fear
3. Listen Deeper, Speak Smarter
4. Question Authority (the right way)
5. Challenge Cultural Norms
6. Write Your Own Script
7. Pursue the Unconventional Path

As a whole, the principles work as a progression, rather than isolated ideas. They move from claiming personal belief and fearless curiosity, to disciplined listening and questioning, and finally toward challenging norms, self-authorship, and unconventional action.

Used together, they will guide you from independent thought to a deliberately lived life.

The following chapters, one per principle, provide examples and an overview of each principle, followed by actionable steps you can take now and on an ongoing basis.

Principle 1:
Claim Your Beliefs

"To be yourself in a world that is constantly trying to make you something else is the greatest accomplishment."

— Ralph Waldo Emerson

The first of the seven principles of Free Thinking establishes the foundation of independent thought. Through thinking for yourself, exercising self-control, and making your own rules, you learn to separate authentic belief from inherited opinion.

Claim Your Beliefs is about ownership—of thought, action, and identity—before the outside world gets a vote.

7
Principles of
Free Thinking
Claim Your Beliefs
Curiosity Without Fear
Listen Deeper, Speak Smarter
Question Authority
Challenge Cultural Norms
Write Your Own Script
Pursue the Unconventional Path

Think For Yourself

Sarah sat in the break room, scrolling through her phone while her coffee cooled. She came across a financial guru whose post promised to turn $5,000 into $50,000 in six months—guaranteed. The comments were wild: half the people called it genius; the other half called it a scam.

Nobody had checked a single source. Sarah felt that familiar tug—the urge to believe something simply because it sounded good.

Sarah wasn't the only one. While she deliberated on this post, three of her coworkers stood nearby, debating which cryptocurrency to buy based on a Tweet they'd seen that morning.

None of them checked a single source.

Let's get something clear before we discuss further. I'm not saying reject all opinions!

There will be times when we unintentionally absorb bad information, but that's okay. We are not perfect!

The challenge is that we live in an era of infinite voices. Social media has democratized opinion to the point where everyone's take feels equally weighted. Scroll through any post—a quote, a news headline, a political statement—and you'll find fifty different interpretations in the comments. Some will sound confident. Some will sound researched. Most will be neither. If you try to absorb them all, you won't become more informed; you'll just become more confused. That confusion becomes a habit. You start doing it on the next post, and the next, and suddenly you're trapped in a rabbit hole where every voice contradicts the last and none of them lead anywhere useful.

The better path is simpler: go to the source. Find the professional, the primary document, or the person who actually has expertise and evidence. Don't outsource your understanding to a comment section. Seek out credible, verifiable information instead of crowdsourced chaos.

Why does this matter?

Some people are dangerously good at sounding right. They can package weak reasoning in confident language. They can make emotional bias sound like logic. Humans are wired to respond to emotion first and evidence second, so these opinions spread fast because they sound convincing. Your coworker reads an article, but doesn't fact-check it. Then he repeats it at lunch because it felt true, and now three more people believe it. Nobody checked. Nobody questioned. The misinformation just traveled.

Plenty of people fall for misinformation, especially when it sounds too good to be true, because they want to believe it.

Take another look at the scam Sarah was falling for. There was a promise to increase the initial investment tenfold because the proposal was about to take the economy by storm, with stocks flying high for a duration of maybe six months.

Will Sarah investigate these false opinions to see if they are genuine? Will she question the credibility of this so-called 'finance guy'?

Would you?

Or do you and Sarah fall for the instant gratification of quick cash?

Questioning, analysis, and figuring out the solution are the best ways to see if this person is a fake or a professional.

Misinformation isn't spread entirely out of unintentional emotional bias; sometimes cruel people lie for financial gain.

So, what do you do?

The antidote is critical thinking.

When someone presents you with information—especially information that promises quick rewards or plays on your emotions—stop. Ask three questions:

- ▹ Who is this person?
- ▹ What's their evidence?
- ▹ What do they gain if I believe them?

A real expert will have verifiable credentials. They'll cite sources. They'll welcome scrutiny.

A pretender will rely on authority ("Trust me, I've been doing this for years), vague promises, or social proof ("Everyone's investing in this"). Pretenders sound smart, and they might be smart.

But sounding smart and being right are not the same thing.

Here's one sentence to carry with you: **An opinion that feels right is not the same as information that is true.**

And if you want to take it further, practice this: the next time someone makes a bold claim in conversation, ask them kindly, and curiously, "where did you hear that?"

Watch what happens.

Most people won't know. And that moment of uncertainty is where real thinking begins.

Key Takeaway

Don't be taken in by uninformed opinions. Only listen to professionals who can back their opinions up with facts. This might be easier said than done, so here are some tips.

Who should you listen to and why?

Picture this: you're scrolling through your phone, and a fitness influencer with perfect lighting and 2 million followers is explaining why you should eat only celery for a week. In the next tab, a registered dietitian with 20 years of experience is explaining balanced nutrition. Your thumb hovers between them. Who gets your attention?

This moment—this split-second choice—happens dozens of times a day in different situations, and it matters more than you think.

Not all opinions are created equal. A personal trainer who's spent a decade studying biomechanics and working with hundreds of clients isn't the same as someone who got abs after three months at the gym. One has expertise—accumulated knowledge, tested methods, and proven results. The other has experience, which is valuable, but limited. Ultimately, you would be wise to listen to a personal trainer's advice on resistance exercise.

However, experts are not infallible. Professionals make mistakes. They carry biases. Sometimes they cling to outdated methods because "that's how we've always done it." This is why it is still a great idea to put your own critical thinking into practice, even after finding a credible source.

After you get a professional opinion, you can conduct your own analysis and do some fact-checking and cross-checking.

When you trust the trainer and show interest in the topic, you can think critically, seeking solutions to get a deeper understanding and value. It's the solution we've all been wanting.

You might listen, but you wouldn't want to take advice from a person who isn't well-informed about a topic, yet still prattles on like they know it all. If you listen and engage, you'll be stooping down to their level, and your critical thinking won't be used wisely.

Most of us seek a professional's advice for the most accurate result. That's why, when you're growing up, your parents say: "hang out with the smart crowd, and you'll gain knowledge; hang out with the wrong crowd, and you'll end up a lowlife with no value to society." (Or words to that effect, anyway.)

What we're saying is to be mindful of whose opinion you take on board.

This applies to any opinion in any conversation—even when it is a simple conversation about your elementary-level times tables.

In fact, it could be about anything. We can recognize credible sources through our own experiences of conducting research.

Education plays a big role in delving into our own research. This is how we analyze evidence to figure out who had the right opinion in a conversation. (And it should come as no surprise that this is normally the person who has researched the information themselves.)

Through our own experiences in life, we connect the dots to figure out truths.

As long as you have a decent education and the wisdom to stick to your beliefs in finding the truth, your critical thinking will continually excel as you continue on your life journeys.

How to filter opinions in daily life

You're sitting across from someone at lunch. They lean forward, voice rising: "everyone knows the economy is about to collapse—my cousin works in finance, and he says it's all rigged." You feel the pull to nod along. It sounds confident enough that you almost believe it. But something in your chest tightens—a quiet alarm that whispers, 'Wait.'

That moment, that pause before you agree or push back, is where your thinking begins.

Every day, you're surrounded by opinions—some informed and some repeated so often they sound like facts. Your mind wants to accept what sounds convincing and move on. But if you do that, you are handing over your judgment to whoever speaks loudest or with the most passion. You stop thinking for yourself.

The first skill in filtering opinions is slowing your reaction. Not for too long—just long enough to ask, do I actually agree with this?"

Bold claims delivered with passion can sweep you along before you've decided what you believe. If you react instantly, you bypass your own judgment and replace it with theirs, which is a disadvantage when discussing something important.

If you're only nodding along to end a conversation you're not interested in, be honest—with yourself and them. Say you need to go.

Here's an important strategy. Pay attention to tone. Is the person speaking with calm confidence, or are they leaning on emotion to persuade you? Manipulative tones often carry urgency, drama, or pressure—you have to believe this. Genuine tones sound resolved, open to questions, grounded. You can feel the difference in your gut. That feeling isn't paranoia; it's your subconscious reading signals your conscious mind hasn't caught yet. Trust it.

Tone reveals intent. Words reveal substance. Sometimes the two don't match. Someone can sound confident while saying absolute nonsense—like a bright yellow car in traffic, it stands out once you're paying attention. Vague language, contradictions, appeals to unnamed "experts" or "everyone knows"—these are red flags. Awareness helps you spot them without effort. You don't need to be a detective. You just need to think critically.

And here's the part many people struggle with: don't be afraid to be skeptical!

If something sounds false, say so. Ask questions; not to offend, but to understand. "Can you explain that more?" or "Where did you hear that?" aren't attacks; they're invitations to clarify. If the person gets defensive, that's on them, not you.

Righteous, respectful skepticism is a virtue, not a flaw.

Have the confidence in yourself to level with them and conclude with the truth; it's that simple. So don't be afraid to say, "I don't know" about someone's opinion; it could save you from being fed some false information.

Have a sense of your own self-awareness. Use it to filter out the junk that some people create in their own heads. Believe and have more knowledge in a positive substance when people are explaining their point of view.

This is where self-awareness becomes your filter. You learn to recognize when someone is guessing but speaking with certainty, when their opinion is shaped more by ego or bias than truth. You also learn to recognize when you're doing the same. The better you know your own tendencies—your biases, your shortcuts, and your blind spots—the better you can separate signal from noise in others.

Body language, tone, and physiology all leak information. It may be a person fidgeting while making a definitive claim. Or someone who won't make eye contact when describing their "sources". You don't need a psychology degree to notice these things. You just need to care enough to look.

You're going to encounter many opinions in your life. Your job isn't to accept them all or reject them all. It's to filter—to let the good in and keep the nonsense out. That only requires awareness. Keep your eyes and ears open, and when someone speaks, ask yourself: Is this true, or does it just sound good?

Think for yourself, but think with evidence

Maya sat across from her younger cousin at a coffee shop, excited to share what she'd learned about nutrition. "You should never eat carbs after 6 pm," she declared confidently. "It turns straight to fat."

Her cousin pulled out her phone. "Where'd you hear that?"

Maya paused. "I ... I think it was a podcast? Or maybe a Tweet from someone?" She felt her certainty crumble. She'd been so sure, yet she couldn't name a single study or doctor, or even remember the full context. She'd been passing along something she'd never actually verified—treating borrowed words as earned wisdom.

That uncomfortable moment taught Maya something crucial: thinking for yourself doesn't mean you stop learning from others. It means you become responsible for what you choose to believe and share.

Ensure that you back up your views with evidence when you are forming and expressing them.

Thinking for yourself comes from learning through our experience, and from people who have influenced us positively.

So when you pass down your knowledge to other people who want to learn your point of view, make sure your sources are credible.

When you began thinking for yourself, it didn't mean you would no longer believe absolutely anybody; it meant you trusted the people who earned their knowledge with evidence.

Why would you want to pass along misinformation to people you're trying to help? I'm sure they also look up to you, given that they came to you for advice. Don't let others or yourself down.

If you make a mistake, it's okay. You can correct it. Even when you do your own critical thinking, always look for the truth; not cynically, but skeptically.

You don't need to dismiss things when you haven't backed up your own evidence. Not only is thinking for yourself backed up with evidence, but it is one of our deepest understandings to gain knowledge. It also elevates us through life when we immerse ourselves in the experience.

People need to realize that learning, failing, understanding, and finding solutions are crucial for our growth and for our success in whatever avenues in life we are trying to do our best in. All great people throughout history have applied thinking for themselves to become better individuals, one day at a time.

So, when you look into your own knowledge from other opinions, while it might be great to trust them, make sure you verify their credibility. Experts can be wrong, especially in science, which is constantly evolving.

Critical thinkers pave the way for deeper perceptions. They listen carefully, paying attention to detail, questioning, and verifying to build their own understanding.

They don't reject all opinions, as that would lead to a total lack of communication. They just reject the ones that aren't backed by truth.

Truth isn't necessarily always out in the open; it waits for the thinker to find it. Therefore, be cautious when you listen to opinions. Remember, it is crucial to heed professionals who are more factual in their field of work, rather than just followers with a slight interest. And, when you explain your opinion to others, ensure that you have solid evidence and facts to back it up.

Try This Now

Next time someone shares a strong opinion—especially on social media—pause before accepting or rejecting it and ask yourself three questions:

1. What's their expertise? Have they studied this formally, worked in this field, or built relevant experience over the years? Or are they just confident?

2. What's their evidence? Are they citing credible sources, or is it all "trust me" and personal anecdotes?

3. Who else says this? Do other credible experts agree, or is this an outlier opinion? Sometimes outliers are right, but they require stronger evidence.

Once you've considered the above, ask the person one clarifying question. This can be any question that tests the claim; your job is to notice how they respond.

Go Deeper

Pick one topic you have a strong opinion about, then actively seek out someone who disagrees with you. Listen to this person's opinion to understand their tone, their reasoning, and whether they're speaking from knowledge or emotion.

You don't have to change your mind, just practice filtering.

Remember This

Your credibility is built one verified claim at a time. Protect it by being honest about what you truly know.

Self-Control

Maria stood in the conference room, hands trembling as her manager reviewed the quarterly report. Three months of work, reduced to a single sentence: "This doesn't reflect our standards."

The heat rose to her face. Her jaw clenched. Every fiber of her body screamed, 'defend yourself!' She wanted to explain away the shortcuts she'd taken, to blame the impossible deadlines. The words were already forming on her tongue when something made her pause—just for three seconds.

In that brief gap, a different question emerged: What if he's right?

Let's elaborate a bit more on self-control and how mastering our emotions and impulses allows us to think more clearly and reach the best possible outcome in any interaction.

Emotions and impulses can interfere with our critical thinking, while self-control fosters an internal discipline that can rectify difficult situations. It's imperative to value this self-control and take it seriously.

Our impulses drive our actions without cause for evaluation; they can bypass our critical thinking process entirely. When this happens, we are led to irrational solutions that don't benefit anyone. To avoid making an impulsive, misguided decision and provide proper solutions, control over ourselves is essential to prevent our minds from being overwhelmed with thoughts that cause negative emotions.

It's not a simple task, but mastery over our impulses is a critical factor in providing others with the right reasoning. This is why we often use the cliché "think before you act." Think of self-control as a gatekeeper, creating a buffer between stimulus and response, and allowing us time for analysis.

When stimulated by a concept someone has told us about, we must have the self-control to analyze the idea and form a proper response instead of being impulsive and jumping straight to a conclusion.

Analysis and evaluation are crucial. Finding a quick answer is not only unlikely to be accurate, but it's simply not a practical way to figure out a solution. When this is your goal, you're pursuing an immediate solution and taking shortcuts.

Be careful with this kind of vice. It is a habit that keeps you ignorant of the truth. It prevents you from growing your mindset.

Ask yourself how you might feel being in a situation like Maria's. How might you react if you were at work and, upon doing a job incorrectly, your boss came to you with harsh feedback on the quality of your work?

Are you the type to act defensively?

Would you prioritize yourself, tell your boss off, and claim your work was good, even though you knew you took shortcuts?

Or would you consider why you were being lazy and see the results of your poor work ethic?

Asking your boss questions to clarify how to do the job properly, instead of just being careless, allows you to get your work done without issues. In most cases, if you need help, your workplace will provide it. However, if your workplace is toxic and doesn't provide help, then you must decide to move on.

Impulses that grow from an emotion that you don't need can affect your thinking for the worse.

Start practicing your self-control so you can make better decisions for yourself, to get your critical thinking working as it naturally should. You'll be better off in the long run; it'll make life easier to understand.

Key Takeaway

Analyze your emotions and impulses before you act. If you start practicing self-control, you'll make better decisions for yourself and develop your critical thinking until it works how it naturally should. You'll be better off in the long run, and life will be easier to understand.

The question is, how do we do this?

How to analyze your emotions and impulses in real time

Sarah's hand hovered over the SEND button. Her manager's email—dismissive, condescending—had landed in her inbox five minutes ago. She'd already typed three paragraphs, each sentence sharper than the last. Her heart pounded. Her face felt hot.

One click and he'd know exactly how she felt.

One click, and she might regret it for months.

She closed her laptop.

Most of us believe that we think, then feel, then act. But the truth runs backwards more often than we'd like to admit. We feel something—anger, fear, excitement—and our thoughts scramble to justify whatever our emotions want us to do. The feeling arrives first. The rationalization follows. Then, by the time we've acted, we're convinced we've made a logical choice.

This is where critical thinking dies—not in ignorance, but in the gap between feeling and action.

Teaching yourself to slow down in that gap is the threshold that brings rational thought back online. The goal isn't to eliminate emotion. Emotions are information. They tell you something matters. But when you let your emotions drive 'the car' without question, you'll end up in places you never intended to go. They're just feelings you need to accept without causing a scene from an emotional eruption.

The first step is to label what you're feeling. Don't say "I am angry," because that fuses your identity with the emotion, as if anger is who you are. Instead, say to yourself, "I feel angry." Just by changing a word, you activate the rational part of your brain and create distance between yourself and the emotion. Suddenly, it's not you, but a feeling you're experiencing. And feelings are transient.

Neuroscience backs this up. When you name an emotion, you engage the prefrontal cortex—the part of your brain responsible for reasoning and self-control. This dampens the amygdala, the alarm system that triggers fight-or-flight responses. In other words, labeling feelings literally calms your brain down.

Labeling alone isn't enough, though. You also need to pause. Not a long, dramatic pause. Not five minutes of deep breathing while everyone waits. Just ten seconds. Count them if you have to. In that brief delay, your nervous system begins to settle. The emotional wave crests and starts to fall. You give your rational mind a chance to catch up.

Once you've paused, ask yourself three questions:

- "When am I feeling this?"
- "What triggered this?"
- "Is my reaction going to help?"

These aren't rhetorical questions. Answer them honestly. Maybe you're feeling disrespected because your manager ignored your input in front of the team. Maybe that triggered old wounds from being overlooked as a kid. And maybe firing off an angry email won't change anything—it'll just make you look unprofessional.

This is critical thinking in real time. You're not suppressing emotion. You're evaluating it. You're choosing a response instead of being hijacked by a reflex.

People respect self-control more than they respect being right in the moment. You might not see it immediately. The other person might still be angry. But over time, they'll remember you didn't escalate. They'll come back. They'll apologize. They'll recognize the maturity it takes to hold your ground without losing your head.

Consider the alternative. A man gets dumped. He's devastated. So he goes out, drinks too much, spends money he doesn't have, picks fights with strangers, and sends texts he'll regret. He's not soothing the pain—he's masking it.

Impulsive behavior doesn't solve problems. It creates new ones.

Healthy self-control doesn't mean white-knuckling your way through life. It means building habits that support your rational mind. Exercise. Work. Spend time with people who ground you. These aren't distractions. They're foundations. Build these, and when the next emotional storm hits, you'll have something to stand on.

Self-control is the healthiest starting point to exercise our critical thinking. It will not only take us ten steps back, but also propel us ten steps forward into healing, whatever adversity we are going through.

When we understand our emotions and urges in the moment, or as they change, we can see the impact we want to make by finding new solutions that help everyone. Don't underestimate these impulses; stay aware.

Building long-term self-control by training your mind

Picture a monk sitting perfectly still in the corner of a monastery as he watches his breath for the thousandth morning in a row.

Now picture a college student who just threw their controller across the room after losing a video game for the third time that night.

The difference isn't talent. It's training.

Our mind is a muscle, but most people don't recognize this. We expect it to perform under pressure without ever putting it through practice. We want self-control in the moment of crisis, but forget that resilience is built slowly, through thousands of small repetitions nobody sees.

Self-control isn't an inherent quality. It's earned through experience—through failing, adjusting, and trying again.

Think of it as callousing your mind. When you lift weights, your hands develop calluses to protect against the friction. When you face difficulty repeatedly, your mind develops its own calluses: patience, resilience, the ability to pause before reacting. Every frustrating moment is an opportunity to build that protective layer.

Be willing to train your mind for a better life outcome, even if you must endure the pain to grow. Meditation and mindfulness are powerful ways of building your self-control for the long term.

When you sit quietly after a stressful day, resisting the urge to immediately grab your phone or turn on a screen, you're practicing something radical: doing nothing when your impulses scream at you to do something. That's the training ground. In that stillness, you learn that your racing thoughts don't control you. You watch them pass like clouds. You realize the panic you felt about today's argument or tomorrow's deadline was real—but also unnecessary and meaningless. What is meaningful is being good to yourself by building that control over your emotions and impulses.

Build your self-awareness of your experiences and take back control of your mind. With critical thinking, find the problem, then solve it.

Journaling

Let's talk about another tool most people underestimate: journaling.

Journaling is an incredible thinking tool. When you write down what happened today and why it bothered you, something interesting occurs: you externalize the chaos. The problem that felt overwhelming in your head looks smaller on paper. Even better, you can now analyze it and find a solution. You can ask: *Why did I react that way? What was I actually afraid of? What would I do differently?*

It may not be easy to be consistent with journaling, but remember that it is just as calming as meditation, so persevering is worth it. When you look back at your journal entries from two years ago and reflect on how none of these problems even exist anymore, those entries become the proof that you'll survive today's problems. You'll realize you're stronger than you think.

When you reflect on how pointless your oversized reactions to your problems are, you will develop self-control in the long term. Keep journaling close to your heart; it's crucial to reflect on your past writing and come up with a solution to your problems that may demonstrate how dimwitted you were, but also makes you grateful for how far your self-control has come.

Think small-scale for a moment

Let's get even more practical. Self-control is also about the micro-decisions you make every single day. Saying no to checking your phone for the hundredth time. Choosing water instead of soda when you're genuinely thirsty, not just bored. Finishing the task you committed to instead of switching to something easier.

These are small wins, but they compound invisibly. Each time you resist a minor temptation, you lay down neural pathways that make the next resistance slightly easier. You're training your brain to tolerate discomfort, to delay gratification, and to trust that you can survive without immediate relief. Over months and years, these tiny victories reshape who you are. You become the person who can walk away from pointless arguments and who can sit with uncertainty without panicking.

The beauty is in the accumulation. You won't notice it day-to-day, but one morning you'll face something that would have destroyed you a year ago—and you'll handle it calmly. You won't even realize how far you've come until someone else points it out, or until you look back at your old journals and see the person you used to be.

Cherish the small wins; they are crucial to building your confidence.

The monk didn't start out calm. The entrepreneur who says no to distractions wasn't born disciplined. The writer who finishes their book despite rejection learned to tolerate discomfort. They all trained themselves, through repetition, through small wins, through looking back and realizing they'd grown without noticing.

You can do the same. Not tomorrow, when the circumstances are perfect. Today, with the messy life you already have.

Why self-control enhances critical thinking and decision making

Two people receive the same harsh email from their boss. One fires back immediately, CC'ing half the company—and, three hours later, realizes they just torched their career over a misunderstanding. The other closes the laptop, takes a walk, re-reads it later with fresh eyes, and responds professionally.

The difference? Self-control. And that self-control didn't just manage emotions—it unlocked better thinking.

Self-control enhances our critical thinking by strengthening the quality of our decision-making and reasoning. It allows us to make more rational decisions rather than rushing to conclusions.

You cannot think clearly when your emotions are hijacking your brain. You cannot reason logically while your ego screams for immediate vindication. Self-control creates the pause—the tiny gap between stimulus and response—where clear thinking actually lives.

Consider what happens in your brain during a heated conversation. Someone says something that triggers you—maybe it feels like an insult or challenges your identity. Your amygdala lights up. Cortisol floods your system. Your prefrontal cortex—the part responsible for reasoning and judgment—is suppressed. You've entered what neuroscientists call an "amygdala hijack." In this state, you're biologically primed for quick, aggressive action, not careful analysis.

Self-control gives your prefrontal cortex time to come back online. You create space for logic to enter the conversation. Instead of blurting out the first thing that comes to mind, you can ask: *What is actually happening here? What does this person really mean? Am I reacting to their words or to my own fears?*

People with weak self-control are extraordinarily easy to manipulate because their emotions sit right on the surface, accessible to anyone who knows how to push the right buttons. Their strong emotions prevent them from realizing they're being manipulated. The manipulator says something designed to make you angry, scared, or defensive, and before you've even processed it, you've taken the bait.

But when you have self-control, manipulation becomes much harder. Why? Because you're not reacting automatically. Someone tries to make you feel guilty, and instead of immediately apologizing or defending yourself, you pause. You think: *Why are they trying to make me feel this way? What are they trying to get from me?* You analyze their tone, their body language, and the timing of their request. You evaluate the evidence instead of just absorbing the emotion they're projecting.

Self-control is critical in a leadership position. Imagine leading a team through a crisis. The deadline is tomorrow, and a key person just quit. Everyone is looking to you, and you can feel the panic spreading. Your self-control will determine the outcome.

If you panic, your team panics. If you make emotional, reactive decisions, you'll make things worse. But if you stay calm, assess the situation logically, and communicate clearly, you'll take the pressure off everyone else.

This maturity is characteristic of self-controlled thinkers. It's a quality that garners respect from others and gives them faith you will get the job done. Self-control can be daunting, especially during a period of struggle. But as long as you persevere, you will grow into a strong leader.

Why you need a personal philosophy

Everyone has a personal philosophy they live by. Some have deep philosophies, while others live by very basic philosophies. It's up to you to decide how meaningful independent thinking will be in adhering to the personal rules you live by.

Most people live by philosophies they never consciously selected. They inherited them from parents, absorbed them from culture, or adopted them from whoever shouted loudest during their formative years. They operate on autopilot, following rules they never questioned, pursuing goals they never examined, living by values they never truly claimed as their own.

Our values are rooted in the beliefs we live by. Everyone has different views of life, whether they are good or bad. It's your life, and you get to choose how you live it. Most importantly, this freedom to think for yourself comes with adulthood. The core values of your philosophy have to mean the world to you; if you live by it, you are being your true self.

The challenge is this: everyone has rules thrown at them by outside influences. Parents tell you how to behave. Teachers tell you what to believe. Friends tell you what's cool. Society tells you what success looks like. The independent thinker's job is to sort through all of it and follow only those rules best suited to their character—not just accept what they've learned from external sources, but look within themselves and create their own principles based on what they've experienced and learned along the way.

Everyone's unique life experiences shape their philosophy. Some people endure pain, suffering, and hardship at a young age. If they choose the right path, their experiences of good and evil will deeply influence their philosophy. When they emerge into the light, they will have profound insights to share with people who don't usually endure serious pain and suffering until they are adults.

Never think a comfortable upbringing will be entirely helpful. Everyone's winter will come one day. No one knows when. But when independent thinkers with deeper philosophies—forged through early suffering—reach the light, they can help those who encounter darkness later. The people who went through hardship at a young age have a duty to guide the newly struggling sufferer through life's pains.

These patterns help independent thinkers express their good qualities, rooted in their personal philosophy, to benefit others.

However, while all the advice in the world is great, a new sufferer fighting their hardest battles should not follow external wisdom that is in conflict with their inner values. They should take the wisdom provided to them and become independent thinkers themselves with a view to elevating their own inner values, not replacing them.

External rules can conflict with inner values. If you're facing philosophies you don't actually stand for, it's hard to grasp when you are going through troubling times. Some people are just too different from us, and this is why independent thinkers need to be around like-minded people. You should surround yourself with people who share similar personal philosophies. It brings more confidence to take ownership of your personal philosophy.

Everyone's philosophy differs. Respect others, even if you don't agree. Make sure they show respect for your philosophy as well. Do not take offense if they are being rude and obnoxious about your philosophies. Have the courage to stand up for yourself at all times.

Finally, accept that your philosophy will evolve. The principles that served you at 20 might not serve you at 40. Growth means letting go of ideas that no longer fit, even if they once felt essential.

Try This Now

Identify your signature impulse—the one that gets you into trouble most often. Is it defensiveness when criticized? Anger when challenged? The urge to have the last word? For one week, every time you notice that impulse arising, pause for five seconds before acting on it.

Keep a simple log: date, trigger, impulse, what you did, outcome. At the end of the week, you'll have data.

Go Deeper

Collect your data over several weeks. You'll start to see patterns in your automatic responses and begin to recognize the cost of letting them run your life. More importantly, you'll be strengthening your gatekeeper.

This small practice will pay dividends in every interaction, every decision, and every moment where your clarity matters more than your speed.

Your impulses will always be there. The question is whether you'll let them think for you, or whether you'll do the thinking yourself.

Remember This

A personal philosophy is the difference between living a life you choose and living one that happens to you.

Make Your Own Rules

Question Everything You Inherited

John's dad is a prominent doctor. He's trying to elevate John by pushing him toward medicine. John knows his father's control isn't always malicious, and that sometimes it comes from love and ambition for his success.

But here's the problem: John's drawn to accounting. He loves numbers and business data.

As he's grown older and started preparing for university, John has found the courage to question what he's inherited. He has realized that controlling others isn't the way, and has decided to think independently, following his own path to become an accountant.

We don't start life as independent thinkers. We start by inheriting beliefs, ideas and ideals. First, we take on our parents' beliefs about success. We're exposed to our culture's ideas about right and wrong. At school, we take on our teachers' assumptions about how the world works.

So, for the first chunk of our lives, we're running on borrowed beliefs, many of which are good because they keep us safe, teach us basic values, and help us navigate a complex world.

However, as we become older, we move toward more independence as thinkers. We ask ourselves whether we really resonate with the core values others have taught us in the past. If we're fortunate enough to have decent parents, their philosophies will have made us better human beings—but we may not agree with everything they say, especially as we gain independence as adults.

This isn't about disrespecting the people who raised us; it's about discovering our own identity and developing our own wisdom and ways of thinking.

Like John, we may decide not to be as controlling as our parents. When we have our own children, we can then guide them in making their own choices—as long as their path is reasonable and leads somewhere meaningful. That's how we learn to think independently: we recognize faults in people's perspectives, and we rectify them with philosophies of a higher quality by thinking about a better way to be.

We should never think of this as discarding everything we've learned. It's about shaping how we truly desire to live by deciding what is worth keeping and what must go.

How do we do this?

Consider these questions:

- What do I consider right?
- What do I consider wrong?
- What sits well with my personality?
- What doesn't sit well with my personality?

The rules you set for yourself create boundaries around how you communicate with people, what opportunities you pursue, and what compromises you make. This is why you can't be one hundred percent the same as the people who taught you from a young age. You are an individual who becomes independent in thinking the way you know how to be. That's why we question everything that shapes us into the thinkers we are and would like to become.

It can be challenging to be truly honest with yourself, especially when you respect the people who raised you. However, that doesn't mean you can't set your own rules by following your personal philosophies. It's a blessing to make your own rules; independence is the road to growth and learning to stand up for what you believe in.

Key Takeaway

Question everything you inherited.

Build your code – define what you stand for

Clarify your core values. These are rules you set for yourself to give your independent thinking the purest meaning of who you are and what you stand for.

Are you a person of integrity, courage, growth, or any other virtue?

Identify the core values that define you; this process brings out your strengths. If you are a person of truth, that's what you must go out to seek. It is the meaning of your existence and why you are here; it's what you stand for.

Maybe you're a fighter: a courageous individual who stands up for themselves and others in perilous situations. Someone who faces down an enemy to uphold true justice and comes out the other end as the hero of the story.

These values serve as your compass. They show you the direction you should move to go wherever life takes you. They encourage you to be a free thinker who shines in your independence as a unique figure.

These values drive growth, but possibly stem from a past of laziness and a lack of seriousness, and are characterized by a lack of responsibility. By adhering to your core values, you could turn your life around and grow into an ambitious person, always learning and helping others improve their lives.

Imagine going from being a person who stays at home in bed, changing the bedsheets every 3 months, to a consistent person of action in line with your philosophy. We learn individual ways of growth by making our own rules to reach the finish line of our journey. We give back to the world by sharing what we stand for. This is how movements start. Being a leader in a positive movement has a significant impact that benefits your purpose.

The rules you impose upon yourself must remain internal. We can spread the word of what we stand for, but there is no room for seeking approval from others about whether our core values are correct or not.

Not everyone will agree with what we stand for. That is exactly why we don't need validation—just acceptance of that reality. There will be people who connect with our beliefs, as long as they are rational and grounded. People who resonate with us should be kept close. They can become lifelong friends. They are the real ones for you.

Your personal philosophy doesn't need to be complex; keep it deeper and personal. The views of your philosophy should be expressed with confidence;

this is when the belief is so strong that it remains unshakeable even when your core values are being challenged.

You know how to stand up for the beliefs that have shaped you into an independent thinker.

Live it – the strength to walk your path alone

They say going against the grain is lonely, but you are never alone when divinity is with you. You walk alone, but you are not lonely; the strength comes from the divine.

The external world sees you as a lonely outcast, and some may even say you're crazy. It's not true; never believe it. The fact is, you're a person of independence, a free thinker who conquers the world in pursuit of living the best life you can.

People will come at you with all they have. They will mock you. They'll say your values are stupid. They'll bully you into giving up what you stand for.

That is not your problem; it's theirs. All you have to do is endure the journey and walk this path alone, facing whatever challenges come your way.

No matter what they are, stick to your beliefs. Stay strong as a person who lives their life to the fullest. Pursue what you love, cherish, and value. People may try to destroy you for your beliefs, but if you are strong enough, they'll never wrench your beliefs away from you. It's all in the mindset, and you're the only one who can decide if you will give in or stick to your faith.

Everyone will have their own experiences, all alone on their path. What most don't realize is that they look too much outward and not enough within. When you do this, you can lose your ability to think independently and conform to social norms. In turn, this leads you to be challenged constantly for being an independent thinker, as you may be more open-minded than others.

Or ... perhaps you're just a courageous person who doesn't care what others think and sticks to the belief you've always had faith in. There is no greater courage in the world than walking a path alone to reveal your true self to the world. We must follow the guidelines in this book to become free thinkers, so our mindset will grow every day, and we get closer to fulfilling our purpose. It's what makes life worth living.

Showing up for yourself every day to strive for greatness is a path where we often struggle with being alone. The real ones endure all the way; those still learning their core values are the ones who usually start again. Never give up on your dream; good work awaits those who build the strength to walk this path.

Know that by living by your own philosophy, you become someone others quietly admire, but more importantly, you respect yourself. An independent thinker becomes their best self by being true to themselves.

This life is temporary; it's best to make the most of it by being genuine and embracing the path we walk alone, without pretending to be someone we're not. It's worth the grand adventure it provides an individual.

Try This Now

Write down one belief you inherited that no longer fits who you're becoming. Then write down what you actually believe instead.

Go Deeper

Look at your new beliefs. Actively make decisions based on the new ones, not the old. Notice what happens—both internally and in your relationships. That's where your real philosophy begins.

Remember This

Walking your path alone isn't about isolation—it's about having the courage to let your inner compass guide you when the crowd is heading in a different direction.

Principle 1 Recap:

Claim Your Beliefs

Core Idea 1: Filter truth from noise—not every opinion deserves your belief.

Core Idea 2: Master self-control—emotions are signals, not commands.

Core Idea 3: Build your personal philosophy—define your own code and live by it, even when you stand alone.

One-liner Reminder: "Think for yourself—but always think with evidence."

Free Thinker Exercise Box

- ▹ **The Belief Test:** Write down three beliefs you'd defend even if everyone disagreed.
- ▹ **Pause Power:** Next time you feel emotional in conversation, take a 10-second pause before responding.
- ▹ **Code of One:** Journal your top five personal values—the rules you choose to live by.

Goal: Strengthen your ability to stand by truth, act with control, and live by your own philosophy.

Free Thinker Challenge (Optional)

Go 24 hours without giving your opinion on anything—just listen, observe, and notice how much noise falls away when you filter for truth.

Principle 2: **Curiosity Without Fear**

"Life shrinks or expands in proportion to one's courage."

— Anaïs Nin

The second of the seven principles of Free Thinking sees curiosity become a disciplined strength rather than a liability. By developing critical thinking, expanding imagination, and surrounding yourself with inspiration, you learn to explore ideas freely without fear of being wrong or constrained by mental limits. This principle opens the mind without losing grounding.

7 Principles of Free Thinking

Curiosity Without Fear

Listen Deeper, Speak Smarter

Question Authority

Challenge Cultural Norms

Write Your Own Script

Pursue the Unconventional Path

Claim Your Beliefs

Critical Thinking

Giselle and Valencia are talking about health supplements.

Giselle says to Valencia, "there's this new natural supplement on the market that cures hair loss in three days. I'm thinking about ordering it."

Valencia doesn't immediately dismiss it, nor does she blindly agree. Instead, she says, "that's interesting. Who published the article?"

Giselle thinks for a moment, then says, "I'm not sure, it was on a health blog."

Valencia frowns slightly and says, "it could be clickbait from a scammer trying to sell false advertising. Were there links to actual studies or research?"

Giselle shrugs and says, "I didn't check, but the author mentioned it had scientific proof."

Valencia pauses, thinking, then says, "you need to look deeper. Just because a blogger writes about something doesn't mean it's true—unless it's backed by facts. And even if it really worked for them, it may not work for everyone else—not unless it's been properly tested."

Giselle nods. "You're right. I didn't think about that."

Valencia continues, "I'm not saying it doesn't work. I'm just saying I'd want more solid evidence before spending money on it."

This dialog between Giselle and Valencia is what critical thinking actually looks like in a real conversation from a critical point of view.

Notice how Valencia was questioning what Giselle told her. She prompted Giselle to give her more information so she could see for herself whether what her friend was saying was grounded in fact, and how much she'd really looked into the topic.

When we channel critical thinking, we change how our thoughts form. We analyze the topic at hand. We evaluate what we've learned during the process. We synthesize it to reach a conclusion based on evidence, rather than emotion or assumption.

This is how we gain clarity.

Once we have used our critical thinking, and we've analyzed, questioned, and evaluated using this way of thinking, the light bulb in our head switches on, illuminating our answer.

Critical thinking is essential for everyday life, work, and home. Everywhere. This form of thinking fosters a mindset that makes us more intelligent when we exercise it in our daily lives for practical purposes.

Key Takeaway

Critical thinking is the mental skill set that separates free thinkers from followers.

Now, let's get to our first set of examples of critical thinking.

Asking the right questions

The right question will lead us toward insight. Asking questions about the topic at hand helps us think more clearly. It is how we gather more accurate information and find the answers we are looking for.

Questions are powerful, but we have to ensure we ask good questions. A good question will spark someone to open their mind to our perspective.

If we stick to questions that are dull and closed, the other party will not consider what we have to say. They will be strongly biased towards their opinion because we haven't convinced them to think outside the box.

So, when you are questioning someone else's opinion, make your questions count. Asking a single powerful question will leave an impact on them and can change their entire perspective. This is where you gain an advantage in determining what is right and wrong. It is how we debate.

In everyday life, we're constantly questioning—at work, at public events, and in casual conversations. Questions are powerful tools for breaking through confusion when we don't understand the other person's opinion.

Here's a simple example: You come home to find your partner is upset about something. You notice they're distant, maybe a little short with their responses. When you ask what's wrong, you receive an explanation, and can then use your critical thinking to attack the problem.

This is how we progress in our compassion toward loved ones. We must first understand before we can succeed with solutions. And understanding comes from asking the right questions.

We challenge assumptions to get a deeper understanding of the truth. In doing so, we uncover the broader difference between right and wrong, and can reach an agreement about which solution is more valid.

When you find yourself in an interesting conversation, make sure you ask good questions to improve the flow of conversation and resonate more easily with the person you're talking to.

What makes a question right?

Consider this scenario. What is the difference between Phil's approach and Geoff's approach?

At a networking event, Phil asks a stranger, "So, what do you do?"

The stranger gives a one-word answer: "Marketing."

Silence.

Phil nods awkwardly. Neither knows what to say next. The conversation dies before it begins.

Meanwhile, across the room, Geoff is talking with a different stranger. "What drew you to your line of work?"

That stranger lights up.

Ten minutes later, they're deep in conversation about career transitions, life philosophy, and lessons learned from failure.

The only difference between these two scenarios is that one person asked a closed question and the other asked the right question.

How do you perceive a question to be right?

See what I just did there? I asked an open-ended question that can transform a dull moment into an intellectual one. Open-ended questions invite deeper exploration, allowing the person you're talking with to resonate with your thinking. If this happens, then both of you will learn something new from each other.

Knowing how to ask the right questions is how we gain respect from others. Practicing good questioning also helps us become more articulate, self-confident, and able to develop a smarter mindset.

Character is built through virtuous habits we practice daily.

We've all been in those shallow conversations that eventually die out. Nobody wants to experience that uncomfortable feeling during an interaction, which is why questioning is so important. We all want conversations with depth.

The "right" question shows you're a human of substance—someone who loves to learn and explore the topic at hand with the person you're talking to. It also gives both participants greater clarity, because asking the right questions allows you to expand on ambiguous ideas.

Sometimes we get lost and misunderstand what someone is saying, so asking the right questions helps us prompt the other person to explain the same idea in a different way that directly addresses our confusion.

The difference between people who just make conversation and people who create genuine connections is questioning. It's not about being charismatic or charming. It's about asking questions that show you see the other person as a complex human being with valuable insights.

Using questions to break mental traps

The right question can help you break others free from mental traps. People fall into these traps with great regularity. Bias can lead people to assume something which is merely plausible is actually an ironclad fact. Bias allows our emotions to draw us to the wrong conclusions.

When we ask the right questions, we're expressing skepticism about the accuracy of what the other person is saying. We're thinking critically about their claims.

Ask questions with humility, not ego. Your goal is not to embarrass people by showing off how much more knowledgeable you are. Be humble. Acknowledge that they may have repeated a claim with good intentions, not thinking they need to look deeper into it.

By asking questions with humility, you not only benefit by receiving the right answer, but you are also presenting the other person with a thought process that helps them probe deeper to find the right answers for themselves.

Try This Now

The next time someone presents you with a piece of information, ask a question like, "Where did you get this information?" or, "What if I said I disagreed with what you just said?"

Go Deeper

Continue to question what other people say to you until it becomes a habit. Then, apply the same questioning to things you hear, read, or believe. Question yourself as well as other people.

Remember This

The quality of your questions determines the quality of your thinking, and the quality of your thinking determines the quality of your life.

Have a Massive Imagination

Author Stephen King draws on his intense imagination to create different stories in the horror genre. Through bringing form to the stories that live in his imagination, King has sold millions of books, and many of these have made their way from paper into feature films. All because of creative thinking.

The story above is one of many real-world examples of how innovative people have used their imaginations as a source of inspiration.

Without the power of our imagination, our minds would be stuck on a single track. We would see only what is—never what could be. But with a vast imagination, it's possible to manifest anything into existence. Our imagination provides us with endless ideas, both good and bad. It is the engine for all our inventions and innovations.

If you are creating an entirely new product, you start by imagining what a great, innovative product would look like.

If you work in a common industry with an established system, your imagination is the key to innovation. It's how you move from the old to the new. This all comes from creative thinking.

Creative thinking is how you generate new ideas, perspectives, and solutions that can be useful to others. And here's the amazing thing: every great idea starts in the mind. Conceptualizing different points of view, picturing scenarios in your head, and creating your own life's work by synthesizing them together—this is the process. Having a big imagination is essential to creating your very own masterpiece, whatever that might be.

The other side to imagination: fantasy

Fantasy and imagination are related, but are also fundamentally different.

Imagination, in the practical sense, is envisioning a realistic concept—something you can eventually write on paper or otherwise bring into existence through action. When you transfer a thought into action, the idea comes alive. Action turns imagination into reality.

Fantasy, on the other hand, is often a way to escape or rest your consciousness, like when you daydream about being a superhero or winning the lottery without any plan to make it happen. Fantasy shows up in art, like paintings and novels. It's valuable for entertainment and emotional exploration, but it doesn't necessarily lead to tangible creation.

Anything can become reality if you truly believe in your creation and take action to bring it to life. If you cannot imagine that something is possible—if you cannot see it clearly in your mind as a potential reality—then you cannot create it.

Key Takeaway

Imagination matters because it's powerful.

Train your mind to imagine – techniques to expand your inner worlds

There are a host of techniques you can add to your repertoire to improve your ability to imagine and use imagination.

Visualize

Visualization is a helpful technique for expanding your inner world. Through focused thinking, you create a picture in your mind that resonates with your interests or explores specific concepts. This isn't just daydreaming randomly—it's using your gift of creativity to conjure up visuals you can bring into your reality.

This is an exercise you should practice daily. If your mind feels foggy and you don't think you have a creative imagination, that's okay. You won't have life-changing ideas every day. The key is consistency. Stay with it. You'll never know when an opportunity will arise from visualizing something amazing.

Daydream

Daydreaming is often seen as a bad thing, but not if you daydream with purpose. There's a difference between productive imagination and escapist fantasy, however, so make sure you're not just daydreaming about something irrelevant that doesn't stimulate you positively. If you're visualizing the specific steps to build a profitable business, for example, that's purposeful.

What if?

Start asking "What if?" This question speaks directly to your curiosity, inviting you to delve deeper into your imagination to seek answers for the ideas you're forming. Curiosity is the part of creative thinking we need to practice with confidence. Curiosity is how you channel your energy into moving forward with the original idea you've conjured.

Read

Embrace the power of reading. Specifically, read fictional books in areas that interest you. Fiction isn't just entertainment—it's imagination training. Gain inspiration from the story. Notice how the author builds tension, reveals character, and solves problems. Then generate your own perspectives. Ask yourself: How could I create something from nothing by being inspired by this approach?

Reading poetry can spark ideas and channel creative thought. Poetry teaches you to see aesthetics in language. You might read a love poem and be inspired to write your own for someone you care about. You might read a poem about loss and suddenly understand how to express the grief you've been carrying. It could be anything that you desire to explore or any talent you want to develop.

Break patterns

This will be tougher but can really elevate your creative thinking. Breaking patterns means trying something new, even for a short time. You'll find it helps you feel more comfortable with new ideas. When you suddenly move off the beaten path, your senses will heighten. Imagination activates most powerfully when we feel slightly uncomfortable, slightly lost, and need to form new ideas to navigate unfamiliar territory.

Simply taking a different route to work makes you more alert and forces you to come up with new ideas for getting there on time.

As simple and tedious as this example sounds, try it when you think you might turn up late. The urgency you feel will activate your imagination and force you to think more actively to get to work on time.

The enemies of imagination – what shrinks your mental universe

Fear of failure

A child builds a tower of blocks. It falls. She rebuilds it, taller. It falls again. She laughs and starts over.

We've all seen this, but fast forward to when this child is thirty. Odds are, she's staring at a blank screen, unable to type a single sentence because it might not be perfect.

What happened?

The enemies of imagination moved in and shrank her mental universe down to a pinpoint. Over the years, she developed bad habits that killed her imaginative thinking. One enemy limiting her is fear of failure.

Fear tells us the cost of trying is too high. It whispers, "what if it doesn't work?" and suddenly your imagination goes silent. You shelve the idea. You tell yourself you'll come back to it later, but you never do.

To defeat this enemy, you must not let it stop you. What's the worst that could happen if you tried anyway? It might not work out. That's not a good reason not to try. Throughout our lives, we will face failure over and over again; we simply need the courage to persevere anyway.

Perfectionism

In my case, the enemy of my imagination was perfectionism. This one will sneak up on you before you realize it. Perfectionism has a way of making you think you're doing the right thing, but the stress and mental fog you'll feel will prevent you from tapping into the full potential of your imagination.

There's a difference between having high standards and being perfect. Having high standards for yourself is great. Putting pressure on yourself to be perfect is not. It's exhausting and slows down your creative process. It drains all your positive energy.

Mistakes lead to opportunities to rectify the issue. They aren't fatal. There's no need for perfection; don't snuff out your ideas before they can fully form, because few things come out perfect the first time.

Blind Acceptance

The third enemy is subtler. It shows up when you trust logic so completely that you stop questioning it. Facts are facts—a combustion engine converts fuel into motion; that's simple physics. But engineers in the 1960s didn't accept that as the final word. They asked, "What if we're thinking about this wrong?" and pushed engines from 100 kilometers per hour to 250, then higher. They used logic as a starting point, then let imagination fill in the gaps.

Don't limit yourself by falling back on modern education as the final answer; use the power of your imagination to see if you can push it further.

Imagination in action — using your mind to build new realities

Imagination becomes useful the moment you stop treating it as separate from action. Every goal you set starts as a mental image—a version of the future that doesn't exist yet. You picture it, then work backwards, making a step-by-step plan to achieve your goal by examining different ideas that might work.

As you form these ideas, your vision grows more meaningful as the problems you are solving start making more sense with each step you take. It's incredible how the mind works. By thinking about ideas in new ways, we can see how they relate, and that's how you arrive at a single, sound idea.

Your imagination enables creative problem-solving, leading you to unconventional solutions.

Consider the following example: for the third time in six months, a thief has robbed a bakery, and now its revenue is down four percent. A conventional way to solve this issue is to install security cameras to identify the thief.

Using his creative thinking, the owner of the bakery comes up with an unconventional solution: he erects enormous signs with the text "CAMERAS EVERYWHERE—YOU ARE BEING WATCHED!" displayed in bold capital letters.

A year goes by with no sign of the thief.

By using his imagination, the owner was able to avoid spending money he didn't have to intimidate the thieves into thinking there were security cameras installed when, in actuality, nothing had changed. Thinking differently helped the company save money.

Imagination isn't a luxury. It's how you grow beyond the limits handed to you and start living a fulfilling life. With this gift, we can bring our ideas into reality and inspire another person. Even if you inspire just one other person, that could give them the spark to turn their life around. That's the biggest blessing you can ask for.

When you inspire another person, your interpersonal connections grow stronger. So embrace your imagination, and use it to change other's lives, not just your own.

Try This Now

Spend an hour each week in your quiet place. Split the hour up over several days if you prefer. Use this time to expand your imagination, visualizing what your life could realistically become.

Go Deeper

Once you've vizualised and created your core concepts in your imagination design a mind map and bring the ideas to life. Use this as a plan to begin the journey.

Remember This

Never underestimate the power of your imagination. You can build empires with it.

Surround Yourself with Inspiration

Shay, a painter, is still trying to find her style. She knows her art is good, but that there's something missing. A spark. On the trip of a lifetime, she visits the Louvre Museum in Paris and finally gets to see the Mona Lisa in person. Instantly, she is struck with inspiration and understands what has been missing in her artwork.

Art can have a major impact, not just on the individual but on a collective. It can cause a ripple effect to change the course of culture. Imagine bringing the art that lives in your mind a reality, and seeing it for yourself. No other dopamine hit can match the feeling of resonating so deeply with the field of painting.

When inspiration strikes, whether it's a painting or something else, your brain doesn't simply receive information; it undergoes a measurable transformation. Dopamine, the same neurotransmitter responsible for motivation and creative problem-solving, floods your neural pathways. It simultaneously loosens rigid thinking patterns while sharpening your sense of possibility. You don't just feel good. You see differently.

One of the strongest dopamine hits you'll ever experience comes from realizing your purpose. The sense of euphoria and inspiration makes anything seem possible. That's how we loosen rigid patterns of thought. It allows us to envision the endless possibilities.

Dopamine hits can also come in smaller, everyday doses, like stimulating the mind through exercise, wellness activities like hot and cold plunges, and a well-balanced diet.

You can also achieve breakthroughs when you bring your feelings and imagination together and become inspired by making an emotional connection. That which inspires you brings happiness and bliss. It gives you this unwavering confidence in your gut that you can create a spectacular work of art to show the world.

It's like when a motivational speaker talks about a topic you have been struggling with, such as fear. The speaker's powerful speech inspires you toward hope and gives you the strength to conquer the fear that has been holding you back. In your imagination, you picture yourself overcoming that fear and building up your confidence to go out into the world and face it for real. When you succeed, your fear will transform into pride and glory.

Remember, feelings that inspire you can fuel your imagination, and you can use this to bring your ideas to life. That's the beauty of how emotions and imagination connect.

Key Takeaway

In a psychological sense, inspiration fuels our creativity. Cultivating a powerful mindset in an environment that fuels creative thought is essential as we draw inspiration from the people, places and art we surround ourselves with.

Design your environment deliberately

Environment doesn't just happen; we have to design and build it. If we do this with intention, our world will spark ideas.

Immerse yourself in an environment that connects

Your physical surroundings matter when you're looking for inspiration. You need to immerse yourself in an environment that connects you to your interests. For example, if you're a musician, go see your favorite local band in person. You can study the way they act on stage and how they get the crowd energised and in the mood. Observe your surroundings. The venue might be chaotic, but everyone is focused on the same thing—the music, and everyone enjoys themselves.

Now contrast that with spending eight hours in a fluorescent-lit office doing work you hate, surrounded by people discussing things that drain you. The first environment sparks ideas. The second dims them.

Spend time in nature

Nature helps clear your mind and bring you to a state of calm, inspiring you to create. The green canopy of trees, the quality of light filtering through leaves, and the quiet away from human noise—these elements help you access your introspection and creativity.

Create an inspirational space

Set up a well-organized office with a minimalist desk, quality stationery, a comfortable chair, and carefully chosen artwork on the walls to help you focus on your inner thoughts. This dedicated space signals to your brain: this is where creation happens. For a writer working on their next novel, this space could be very inspiring—a place designed specifically to help ideas flow from mind to paper.

Don't forget your digital environment

Your digital environment matters just as much as your physical one.

In the age of social media, billions of people scroll through feeds designed to distract them and keep them on the platform—and away from their lives. To get daily inspiration, you need to curate deliberately. Follow creators, thinkers, and innovators whose work challenges you. If you're a doctor, follow renowned physicians. If you're a scientist, follow researchers doing novel work. You'll naturally follow family and friends, but avoid filling your feed with egotistical people who flaunt their material wealth or hollow content designed purely for low-brow engagement and shock value. These accounts don't inspire. They discourage. They make you feel less creative, not more.

Avoid negative people

The same principle applies offline. Negative people—the chronically uninspired, the perpetual complainers, those who mock ambition—drain your creative energy. You don't need to be cruel, but you do need to be selective about who gets regular access to your attention. That cluttered noise will destroy your creativity if you let it.

Design your environment with care; you don't need to accept what diminishes you when you have the power to change it. The choice is yours.

People are catalysts, so seek inspired company

The people around you shape your thinking, whether you realize it or not. They influence your ambitions, your standards, and your creative capacity through both conversation and example.

This works in two directions. Inspiring people elevate you through their energy and ideas. But uninspiring people also teach you something—they show you exactly what you don't want to become. When you observe someone stuck in bitterness or paralysed by doubt, their misery can catalyse your own change. You see their life as a warning and adjust your path accordingly.

Seeking inspiration can begin with surrounding yourself with people who actively build things.

Picture this: you're sitting with friends who share your ambitions—you could be bandmates writing your next hit song, or co-founders developing a startup. The conversation flows. Someone throws out a half-formed idea, another person builds on it, and a third sees a connection no one else noticed. You're jotting down all your ideas and refining the vision together. By the end of the conversation, everyone's energy has come together to inspire a concrete plan that will bring these ideas to life.

This is why it's so important to surround yourself with the right people.

A student earning a B+ who wants an A+ doesn't study with unmotivated classmates who don't care. He gravitates toward the students who treat academic achievement seriously. Ambitious people will inspire ambition in you in turn.

Valuable people create value for you. They have a brilliant sense of curiosity, which leads them to ask better questions. They express themselves authentically, which is an important trait to have. If your current friends don't inspire you, find better company.

One of the most powerful relationships you can build is with a mentor—someone ahead of you in your craft who has already navigated the challenges you're facing. The right conversation with the right mentor can trigger breakthroughs that save you years of trial and error.

Eventually, you may surpass your mentor; it is up to you how far you take it. Just make sure that spark of inspiration never dies; keep thinking creatively and look for unique ideas to level up your career and life's work.

Surround yourself with builders, not just dreamers who don't act. They may come up with brilliant ideas, but if they're too lazy to build them, it's a waste of time. Their energy can even be corrosive, eating through your creative energy. Don't let anyone take your energy.

Creative rituals of inspiration

Inspiration doesn't follow a schedule, and so it's essential to make inspiration an active daily practice.

You need to engineer the conditions to make inspiration more likely to appear. That's where rituals come in. Rituals are deliberate practices you return to consistently, training your mind to recognize creative patterns and generate ideas.

Everyone has their own set of positive habits that inspire them.

Go for a walk

A popular ritual for the average person is a simple walk. Don't take your phone or any other device likely to distract you, as this will cloud your creative thinking. Just getting your heart rate up and letting your blood flow activates your cardiovascular system. Because the body and mind are connected, this is far more conducive to creativity than sitting at home with your thoughts. You're stimulating your body, which in turn stimulates your mind.

Listen to music

Listening to music can also be helpful. The right album—one that taps into your emotional frequency and resonates with your current state—can jumpstart your creativity. Just keep listening, and you'll find music that will help you, no matter which genre you prefer.

Travel

If you have the finances, traveling to foreign countries is a more exciting, short-term way to gain inspiration. Seeing how people from other cultures, especially those less fortunate, go about their daily lives will help you cultivate gratitude. It can be both humbling and inspiring to experience firsthand how many more opportunities you have than someone with a poorer lifestyle.

Even a week-long road trip around your own country will give you the chance to set up a daily ritual. Driving past changing landscapes creates natural moments for reflection. Observe the scenery around you and let your mind wander. Your brain will naturally form new connections. You never know what spark of inspiration will strike you. You'll return home seeing your life differently, with a fresh perspective on problems that seemed intractable before you left.

Be intentional

Intention matters more than location. When picking out a movie, look for more than pure entertainment value; make time to watch something more meaningful. It's okay to watch a silly movie for a laugh; fun is important. Just make sure you balance entertainment with movies that inspire you. Watch something meaningful that will make you think differently.

This also applies to podcasts, books, plays—anything that taps into your imagination. Go out into the world and find your spark through your custom-made rituals.

Try This Now:

Regularly surround yourself with sources of inspiration to stimulate your subconscious mind into generating new ideas. (You never know when you might have that life-changing idea that changes the world—like Steve Jobs did with the Macintosh.)

Go Deeper

Audit your surroundings. Walk through your workspace and remove anything that doesn't serve focus or inspiration. Review your social media and unfollow ten accounts that drain rather than energize you.

Create one weekly ritual—a visit to a gallery, a walk in nature, a live performance—that reliably sparks ideas. Make it non-negotiable.

Remember this: You become the average of the people you spend time with. Choose wisely.

Principle 2 Recap: Curiosity Without Fear

Core Idea 1: Curiosity is the engine of growth — it pushes you to question what others accept.

Core Idea 2: Asking the right questions sharpens your mind and deepens your understanding.

Core Idea 3: Imagination turns curiosity into creation; fearless inquiry transforms ideas into innovation.

One-liner reminder: *"Fearless curiosity is the lever that moves the world."*

Free Thinker Exercise Box

- ▹ The Daily Question Drill: Each day, write down three "what if" questions about something you saw or read.
- ▹ Flip the Frame: Take one assumption you believe and ask the opposite question– "What if this wasn't true?"
- ▹ Curiosity Conversations: Find someone with a different perspective; ask five questions without defending your own view.

Goal: Strengthen your courage to ask better questions and explore without fear of looking foolish.

Free Thinker Challenge (Optional)

Spend a full day asking "Why?" at least five times before accepting any answer. Do this about work, media, and general conversation. Notice how your perspective expands.

Principle 3:
Listen Deeper, Speak Smarter

"Most people do not listen with the intent to understand; they listen with the intent to reply."

— Stephen R. Covey, *The 7 Habits of Highly Effective People (1989)*

The third of the seven principles of Free Thinking refines awareness and judgment. Emotional intelligence, reflection, and solitude teach you to observe before reacting, to process before speaking, and to listen beyond surface-level noise.

Clear thinking begins with quiet attention.

7 Principles of Free Thinking

Claim Your Beliefs

Curiosity Without Fear

Listen Deeper, Speak Smarter

Question Authority

Challenge Cultural Norms

Write Your Own Script

Pursue the Unconventional Path

Emotional Intelligence

Steph is arguing with her co-worker about how to complete a project. Thinking she was helping, Steph's co-worker had offered her opinion and some advice. Steph, who was already stressed, did not appreciate her co-worker's input, feeling it was judgmental rather than helpful. What started as respectful communication quickly escalated into a heated discussion with increasingly inflammatory language.

Emotions are natural. We all experience them. It's part of being human. But emotions, particularly negative ones, can obstruct rational thought when you need it most.

In tense situations like the one between Steph and her co-worker, our judgment can become clouded, completely blinding us to the other person's words.

This is the battle between emotion and logic. When emotion dominates, we stop thinking critically. We don't question why we're so reactive. We don't search for resolution. We simply react, which rarely leads anywhere productive.

Someone with high emotional intelligence will ask clarifying questions when communicating with others. They will analyze the issue at hand rather than try to defend their ego. Their aim is to reach a conclusion both parties can understand and accept.

Sometimes the other person won't—or can't—tone down their emotions. That's when we must be the ones to extend empathy. While it is difficult to drop our pride, if we genuinely want to understand the other person's perspective and have them understand ours, we must be humble.

When tension begins to rise in a discussion, that's our cue to activate our emotional intelligence. We need to question whether our feelings are helping us think clearly—or preventing us from doing so.

We can't believe everything we feel.

Criticism is a case in point. Rather than reflecting on criticism received, many people respond defensively. However, people with emotional intelligence are able to examine criticism for truth, even when it's delivered poorly or offensively.

Critical thinking helps us grow into a better version of ourselves in all aspects. Thinking critically provides the tools to navigate conflict. We learn to stay calm under pressure. We become attuned to others' needs and perspectives, not just our own.

This is how the principles of free thinking help us become the person we long to be.

The reputable free thinker always comes out on top. Despite losing many battles, the free thinker can still rise above it all.

Key Takeaway

Learn how to analyze and control emotions so they work for you rather than against you.

Mastering self-awareness

Self-awareness is a critical weapon, but to be able to benefit from it, you must learn to use it properly. This means knowing your emotional triggers and recognizing when your emotions are hindering your critical thinking. If you can learn to recognize these, you can then respond thoughtfully rather than reactively.

Start by identifying your emotional patterns. Ask yourself the following questions (and answer honestly):

- Do I get anxious when challenged?
- Am I easily offended when I'm wrong?
- Am I afraid that confrontation might lead to violence?

These questions reveal what holds you back. Often, defensive reactions stem from emotional bias—a refusal to accept truths that threaten your self-image or beliefs. Recognizing this pattern is the first step toward changing it.

The hardest part of self-awareness is being willing to look past your ego to accept your faults. It can be hard to let go of an idea you desperately want to believe despite it not being true, or to give up on a damaging ideology simply because it is familiar to you.

Mastering self-awareness is key. Even if you are wrong, having the self-awareness to finally accept this doesn't make you any less of a person. In fact, it shows courage. It demonstrates that you value facts more than your ego, which leads you towards strength. This is a major step in personal growth.

There are several techniques you can practice to increase your self-awareness.

Journaling

Keeping a journal is one of the most effective methods of increasing self-awareness. When you react poorly to a situation, open your journal. Don't try to justify your actions; just write about the incident and how you responded.

Once you've written the facts objectively, analyze them. Ask yourself why you reacted in that way. What emotion was driving your actions?

This process—writing then analyzing—helps you evaluate your emotional intelligence. Once you understand your patterns, you can think about how you could respond to similar situations in the future. You might even apologize to the people involved, which helps ease the tension and restore harmony.

Pause first

When emotions run hot, our first impulse is rarely the best response. Pausing before reacting can completely shift our emotional state.

The result is incredible. That brief pause can transform an argument into a productive conversation. It allows us to process how we feel before we respond. A principle we should all remember is that we cannot think for ourselves if we don't know what we feel.

Our ability to communicate deteriorates when we're overwhelmed by multiple emotions simultaneously. This can lead to being unable to get our point across effectively, and, worse, saying something we later regret.

Self-awareness requires consistent practice. As you develop it, you'll discover flaws in your thinking, but that's the beauty of it: our imperfections, driven by limited emotional intelligence, become visible. And once they're visible, we can address them and become a better thinker and person.

Emotional regulation

Maintaining a sense of calm allows us to think clearly and maintain self-control. Yet, being calm is a very underrated state of being that many people struggle to attain.

Regulating emotions is not about suppressing them; it's about not letting them dictate our actions.

When we are in a state of calm, we're grounded—even if we are feeling negative emotions. Remaining calm is always the best option when faced with conflict. Allowing ourselves to be carried away by our emotions only adds fuel to the fire. It's like having the devil on your shoulder.

Nobody wants to react poorly at work and then go home feeling upset. We don't want to inflict our negative energy on others. However, people with high emotional intelligence can respond to tense situations by keeping calm and working through issues logically and in a civil manner.

We need to acknowledge, however, that this is easier said than done.

In the heat of the moment, our immediate emotional reaction may seem justified—even though it isn't—but avoiding the pull and remaining calm will instead allow you to respond as you wish you had later on.

This kind of emotional self-control develops through mental discipline, which is, in turn, obtained through first-hand experience.

Think back to when you were a teenager. How did you handle conflict back then compared to how you handle it now, as an adult? There would be a dramatic difference—or at least I hope so!

Critical thinking accelerates this development as you mature. It allows us to approach situations by:

- questioning our emotional responses
- analyzing why we felt this way
- evaluating whether our reaction was proportional
- developing better strategies for next time.

Following these steps allows you to build the mental discipline that strengthens emotional self-control.

The mind, when calm, allows you to see clearly. When a prominent CEO is in a board meeting, on the cusp of closing a major deal that will give the company a massive breakthrough, he must remain calm and use his emotional intelligence to seal the deal.

If he allows himself to become reactive, he stands to lose not only the respect of his clients but the deal as well. Remaining calm will give him the upper hand. It will show that he is a professional with an abundance of confidence and demonstrates the company's competence to succeed with the deal.

It takes time to learn to remain calm under pressure, but it is a very effective tool for handling countless situations.

You never know when remaining calm may save your life or even create your dream life.

Empathy without absorption

To think critically, one must understand other people without getting lost in their emotions and becoming reactive. This requires empathy, but empathy that sharpens your thinking rather than weakening it.

Empathy is the ability to see another person's perspective with clarity. Having empathy helps us really hear the words someone is saying and understand why they're saying them. With strong empathy, we can also pick up on what people aren't saying. We can find out more about a person by analyzing their body language, physiology, and facial expressions—even their tone of voice.

For example, if someone you're talking to is tensed up, has a stressed facial expression, and is speaking in an agitated tone of voice, your emotional intelligence should be sounding alarm bells. This person's needs are evident: they need you to hear them out and calm them down by helping them find a solution to their problem.

On the flip side, not everyone who claims to be empathetic actually cares about the other person. In fact, empathy is the favored tool of manipulators. After all, manipulation only works when you understand your target.

Empathy is a powerful tool, so use it to help people rather than for self-gain. Who knows ... you could even save someone's life by giving them the understanding they desperately needed in a critical moment.

In addition, remember that empathy can also be used to protect yourself from others. Be wary of manipulative people, as they will drain your energy by exploiting your kindness for their own personal gain. If your empathy tells you that someone is attempting to manipulate you, don't lose your head. Make an effort to help them, but know when to walk away. Your energy is finite, so save it for yourself and for people who really need your help.

Don't confuse empathy with weakness. If someone mistakes your kindness for vulnerability, defend yourself clearly. Set boundaries. Show strength. Empathy is not a soft trait—it's how you build character and develop humility while maintaining your own integrity.

Try This Now

Next time you're involved in a confrontation, take time afterwards to write down the negative emotions you and the other person felt.

Go Deeper

Examine those emotions. Think about them and consider how the situation could have been handled in a more mature manner without getting out of hand. Repeat this process as needed while working toward applying this thinking during the situation.

Remember This

You can control your emotions and make them work with and for you.

Reflect

A personal reflection: When I began my journey toward free thinking, I struggled to analyze my experiences—how I reacted to them, what I learned from them, and how to build resilience to overcome adversity.

Looking back, I'm in awe of how much I've grown through my struggles, losses, and heartbreaks. Each challenge, each thing I struggled with, taught me to treat people better. The self-examination I conducted—and still conduct—daily has made me wiser and continues to bring clarity to my life, granting me peace even amid the chaos of our busy society.

Self-examination is the foundation of reflective thinking. Through this examination and reflective thinking, you can shape your ability to think independently and become a free thinker.

In short and simple terms, regular practice of reflective thinking makes you a better person.

Reflecting on our lives allows us to examine events we may not have fully processed. We can start at any point we desire. We could reflect on a traumatic experience that took years to overcome. We might calmly consider, for instance, how a fear of heights has stopped us from riding on airplanes for five years. After finally overcoming that fear, we can later reflect on the strength required to push through, even if it took five years. It can give us the strength to get through our current struggles.

By reflecting on how we've overcome adversity, we show ourselves how resilient we really are. It's tangible proof we can make it through whatever we're currently struggling with, because we've faced worse before.

Without reflecting, we cannot know that we may be happier, wiser, or more capable than we were a decade ago. We remain blind to that growth. Even during rough patches, reflection reveals that life is rarely as bleak as we imagine.

Those who never self-examine will live their lives without ever truly knowing themselves. That's when all your negative emotions take over, trapping you in a cycle of stagnation rather than growth.

Self-examination is essential for finding purpose, inner peace, and direction. Don't let modern life distract you from discovering your true self. This practice leads you toward your destiny.

Key Takeaway

Socrates said, "The unexamined life is not worth living." Without reflection, we cannot appreciate our progress or how far we've come.

Techniques for deep thought

Everyone has their own methods for delving deep into their mind. Let's talk about how we can use some of them to channel reflective thinking and find answers about ourselves.

Solitude

When no one else is around, we have the space to reflect on our past successes and access the positive emotions associated with them. Solitude allows us to find inner peace. We use this time to gain clarity and motivate ourselves to move into the next phase of our lives.

If we want a more empowering journey of self-reflection, solitude is perfect. It can happen anywhere: during a walk without our phone, while sitting alone in a café observing our surroundings, or while traveling. Travel particularly supports self-examination because it removes us from the structured routines of work, family, and socializing. A quiet environment naturally leads to more reflective thinking, and with time on our hands, we can focus on our free thinking and the road ahead. It's a blissful experience.

Meditation and mindfulness

Slowing our thinking allows us to see more clearly. Different religions approach meditation in different ways.

As a Christian, I like to sit in silence and meditate using the Jesus prayer. I sit in a comfortable position, in complete stillness, and repeat the prayer silently in my mind: "Lord Jesus Christ, Son of God. Have mercy on me, a sinner." This prayer reminds me that God shows kindness to sinners like myself who will never be perfect like Him. Through this practice, I gain the clarity to examine what I need to let go of from my past, knowing God will show mercy.

The Buddhist monks also have powerful meditation techniques to cultivate mindfulness. They sit in stillness in quiet temples, chanting while incense burns to create a calm atmosphere. Through these practices, they find inner peace.

Spirituality helps us discover ourselves and find inner peace through mindfulness techniques. That's also the beauty of religion in general.

Facing the inner mirrors

Self-reflection isn't always easy. Confronting difficult truths and unresolved emotions from our past can feel overwhelming, especially when we're struggling in the present. This is a tough road, as we often deny who we are out of fear of who we might become.

This isn't about being hard on yourself. It's about accepting what has happened in the past so you can heal and move forward. Facing your inner mirrors is about growing as a person by letting go of your fears, doubts, and past traumas.

Being honest with ourselves causes discomfort, which is why most people avoid it. Our egos try to protect us from painful self-awareness, causing us to reject reflection entirely and numb ourselves with bad habits. This is how people turn to drugs, alcohol, and other toxic addictions. The discomfort is most intense in the beginning, and many people can't handle it, but if we endure, the process can be life-changing, and we can become who we're destined to be.

Emotional intelligence is a great tool for self-reflection. It helps us understand our traumas and how we have reacted, both during the horrible situations and in the aftermath. Patterns will emerge in the traumatic experiences we overcame, and we will see how we found the courage to keep moving forward.

Confronting these issues isn't easy.

I didn't begin serious self-reflection until I was thirty, during my first year of recovery from drugs and alcohol. But once I accepted my past and understood that it didn't define who I am now, the experience became liberating.

It is the same for others. For example, someone struggling with jealousy can examine the root of that feeling through reflective thinking and can transform that darkness into growth.

The more we face the inner mirrors on the road to self-discovery, the stronger we'll be when it comes time to accept the truth and move on.

Turning reflection into action

Ashley had begun treating coworkers aggressively in his new role as a supervisor. After some time, he realized he was in a constant state of anger, and it was leaving him stressed.

Through self-reflection, Ashley realized he was treated aggressively when he started. He'd assumed such behavior was normal.

Recognizing this pattern, Ashley was able to drop his ego and become more empathetic. As a result, he was less stressed, calmer, and, most importantly, he was able to maintain a healthier work environment. As the supervisor, Ashley is now merely firm with his subordinates without being harsh, and, as a result, productivity began to improve.

Letting go of past experiences that hold us back is helpful, but for the insights gained from that reflection to be useful, they need to translate into action. Reflection without action is only rumination. If Ashley had only noted that he was treated the same when he was a new recruit and hadn't changed his own behavior, his self-reflection would have been meaningless.

Self-reflection doesn't need to produce life-changing results every day of our lives, but when it is a consistent part of our lives, we will no longer be the type of person who lets all our negative traits accumulate and settle into our subconscious. When we ignore our feelings and tell ourselves everything will be okay, it only leaves us empty.

Self-examination directs us toward a life of abundance and fills our empty minds with quality thoughts.

Try This Now

Choose one area of your life that has been bothering you and work on channelling your inner awareness into external behavior. Notice when other people notice the change.

Go Deeper

Build self-reflection into your daily practice. Fifteen to thirty minutes a day is recommended to see improvement.

Remember This

Reflective thinking only changes your life when you act on it.

Solitude

Nathan was always telling people how busy his life was, and it was true. When he wasn't working for and with clients, he was working on his business—invoicing, answering emails, and social media. On the rare occasions he had time to himself, he always found something to do that involved his business.

Over time, Nathan became less productive. His to-do list was long and he never seemed to get to the end of it. He didn't know what was wrong and couldn't understand why he was losing clients. He resolved that he'd just have to work harder, longer hours. He also engaged a very expensive business coach, hoping to get some answers.

Eventually, his partner noticed. "Just stop," she said. "Take a walk. No devices. Spend time with yourself."

Nathan thought it was a ridiculous idea, but she insisted. He went for a walk for half an hour. In that time, alone, without distractions, he unravelled a problem that had been bugging him for months. He tried it again the next day with a similar result.

Now, Nathan builds time into each workday to stop and reflect.

Solitude has the power to nourish our soul and mind. It gives us the space to declutter our minds and delve deep into our thoughts. Intentional solitude is not isolation or loneliness—it's a deliberate choice to remove ourselves from distracting environments and negative emotions. When we do this, we're able to calm down, think more clearly, and find solutions to our current problems.

Most people don't appreciate the benefits of solitude. We chase constant stimulation and look to others for advice rather than finding the answers ourselves through reflection. Reflective thinking in solitude often leads to better answers because we understand ourselves more deeply than anyone else can.

Digital consumption is a big distraction for many people today. It leads to information overload, which is antithetical to clear thinking. We often find ourselves glued to our phones, inane information clogging up our brains as we scroll past. We'll read about someone who bought a new car, or a famous person who bought a new house. It's too much.

The issue isn't the content itself; it's the level at which we are forcibly inputting information into our brains and overstimulating ourselves. It leaves us exhausted because we're using so much energy, and it stresses us out because our brains feel compressed by all the information we're weighing it down with.

Solitude is the key to decompressing and clear thinking, and it leads to all kinds of benefits. Without those distractions, we have room for higher-quality thoughts, and we feel physically healthier. We have more energy, and we find ourselves in a better mood as a result.

Solitude also cultivates original thinking, allowing us to examine our lives from our own perspectives rather than relying entirely on the viewpoints of others.

Solitude is not weakness—it's strength.

Key Takeaway

There is power in solitude. People who spend time alone demonstrate resilience and self-respect.

Deep thinking

Unlike shallow thinking, which doesn't provide real solutions as it only addresses the problem at the surface, deep thinking allows us to move beyond surface-level awareness. Through deep thought, we seek a thorough understanding of the issue at hand, and can find meaningful answers that produce the best results.

Deep thinking is an exploration of the mind that requires a tolerance for discomfort, patience, and uncertainty.

While it is uncomfortable to set aside our biases and face difficult truths, it's essential if we are to move on from whatever we're going through. If we only approach our problems with shallow thinking, we'll never get to the root of the problem, and we'll keep making the same mistakes. The lesson keeps repeating until we sit down, accept the truth, and take action to overcome the problem.

Many people say they lack time for solitude, but the truth is that they overestimate how time-consuming it is. Solitude doesn't require spending months away from regular life. We need only set aside a brief period of our day to spend time alone in reflection. "I'm too busy" is not an excuse. Not even billionaires are that busy. It doesn't matter who you are; everyone needs time alone, even if only in small amounts.

Deep thinking has become rare today because modern technology has heavily distracted society. We continuously scroll through fast-paced content on social media to kill time, and it can shatter our attention spans. Free thinkers don't waste their spare time on distractions like this every day.

Imagine being in an important meeting, but you aren't paying attention to a word your boss says because you're distracted by your phone. You'll need to approach him after the meeting to ask him to repeat himself. Prepare yourself to look foolish.

At a more fundamental level, this level of distraction leaves you empty and prevents you from finding the quiet of solitude to reflect on yourself and the uncertainties in your life.

Solitude and deep thinking work together powerfully. Solitude provides the silence necessary for a peaceful, attentive state of mind, which enables deep thinking. Without distractions, your mind becomes active and engaged.

Make time for deep thought to gain quality insights—shallow thinking should not dominate your life.

Using solitude to understand yourself

The inner journey is a world of beauty, pain, wisdom, and heartache—all the positive and negative emotions that make us human. Through this journey of self-discovery, we can see different versions of ourselves from the past, how we've evolved, and where we're traveling now.

Solitude creates the stillness required for self-examination. To be still is to let go of the external world and look within. We cannot see ourselves clearly when we are always in motion. Stillness guides self-examination, and solitude is the key to achieving it. Solitude reveals what distractions hide, bringing us toward truth rather than leaving us in a state of overthinking.

It may be confronting to sit in solitude, but it uncovers important truths. Hidden fears can be hard to face, but can be life-changing. Solitude is the basecamp for exercising reflective thinking. Letting go of desires we haven't yet achieved can be frustrating, especially when they're only just out of reach. Self-reflection can help us find the root causes of these struggles.

Many people need to develop patience or commit to consistent hard work first, rather than seeking instant gratification. We all want things, and we want them quickly, but life doesn't work like that. Solitude provides the space to discover the tools and techniques needed to achieve what we desire over the long term.

As difficult as self-reflection can be, especially when it comes to finding the time to be alone and start working on our free thinking, we must resist the urge to flee. Many people avoid solitude because it forces them to confront past traumas, emptiness, and regrets. It has to be seen as healing and not a danger to run from. The total acceptance of oneself is one of the most important answers in our inner journeys.

Vision and Originality

Self-reflection allows us to build a mind that sees beyond the moment. Not only can we uncover truths, but we can also envision how far we can go in life once we have let go of what holds us back. This is how free thinkers constantly elevate their personal journey of self-discovery. Solitude creates the conditions for seeing what others don't, whether that is in our personal lives or taking our career to the next level.

By providing a quiet space to clear our minds and think deeply, we can develop vision. Others spend their time in chaos, never finding meaningful answers amid constant distractions. Without a peaceful, serene environment, we don't have the time and breathing space to look at the bigger picture. This means we can only get short-term answers because we're only responding to what's urgent.

True vision requires distance from the crowd; a quiet place of stillness. Original thoughts play a big part in being a free thinker, and solitude provides the silence to let them flourish. Without second opinions—even if we think they're better than what we can come up with—we develop independence and self-reliance.

Stop following others' thoughts and start hearing your own. This is how we gain confidence in our ability to think freely. Many great thinkers throughout history—Marcus Aurelius, Einstein, Thoreau—spent long periods of time in solitude where they developed their best ideas. Their work is proof of the power of reflective thinking. If they could use it to grow their own mindsets, so can you.

A visionary mindset in solitude allows you to think long-term. It will detach you from the urgency of now and let you think in decades rather than days. When we get caught up in the moment, we become so stressed by the urgency we create. Self-reflection in solitude helps us refocus on the long-term vision, decompressing from a high-paced mindset and recognizing that success is a long game. If you need to change direction to achieve your vision more smoothly, solitude provides the clarity to make that choice.

Try This Now

Spend thirty minutes completely alone right now. Go to another room or outside. Leave your phone and other distractions behind. Just be. Notice where your thoughts go.

Go Deeper

Schedule in time for solitude every week in the same way you would schedule an appointment. This is a meeting with yourself. Make yourself do this until it becomes a habit—if you miss it, you will feel out of sorts. Use the time intentionally to reflect, ask questions and analyze answers.

Remember This

Solitude will give you the environment to expand your knowledge and understanding. Use it wisely

Principle 3 Recap:

Listen Deeper, Speak Smarter

Core Idea 1: Master self-awareness — know your emotional triggers before they control you.

Core Idea 2: Respond, don't react — calm thinking creates better outcomes than heated emotion.

Core Idea 3: Lead with empathy — listen beyond words to understand others without absorbing their chaos.

Core Idea 4: Reflect and reset — use solitude and journaling to turn emotional noise into insight.

One-liner reminder: *"Feel deeply, think clearly, and speak wisely."*

Free Thinker Exercise Box

- **The Pause Practice:** When tension rises, pause for 10 seconds before responding. Notice how calmness changes clarity.
- **Trigger Tracker**: Journal a recent emotional reaction. What sparked it, and what could you have done differently?
- **Empathy Lens:** In your next conversation, focus only on understanding the other person's point of view—no fixing, no defending.

- **Solitude Session:** Spend 15 minutes alone each day reflecting on your emotions and what they're teaching you.

Goal: Strengthen emotional intelligence, listen with intent, and respond with wisdom, not impulse.

Free Thinker Challenge (Optional)

Spend one full day observing your emotions like a scientist. Don't act on them—note what you feel and why. You'll start to see how calm awareness transforms your conversations and decisions.

Principle 4: Question Authority (the Right Way)

"Children should be taught to question everything. To question everything they read, everything they hear. Children should be taught to question authority. Parents never teach their children to question authority because parents are authority figures themselves."

— George Carlin

The fourth of the seven principles of Free Thinking teaches discernment over defiance. By recognizing cognitive bias, avoiding emotional manipulation, and staying open to changing your mind when faced with better evidence, you learn to challenge ideas responsibly—without ego, bitterness, or blind rejection.

7
Principles of
Free Thinking
Curiosity
Without
Fear
Listen Deeper
Speak Smarter
Question
Authority
Challenge
Cultural Norms
Write
Your Own Script
Pursue the
Unconventional
Path
Claim
Your Beliefs

Recognize Cognitive Bias

Bryan has been boxing from a young age. He had some success as an amateur and has recently moved into the professional circuit. He's always looking for opportunities to fight and rise in the rankings so he can achieve his ultimate goal of becoming world champion.

One day, he sees a call to go up against a long-standing champion who has multiple wins to his name. As a pro-boxer, Bryan only has four professional fights under his belt, yet he decides to go for it, believing he is experienced enough to challenge the champion.

He's not. He gets knocked out in the first round. Undaunted, he puts himself forward again, in a similar situation, the following month. The result is the same, but Bryan brushes it off with excuses. He repeats this pattern over and over, still believing he is ready, and he just hasn't had the right opportunity yet.

Cognitive biases are patterns that lead to unhealthy thinking. They stem from one-dimensional perspectives and a failure to consider alternative viewpoints that may be more accurate than our own. We become so attached to our beliefs that we refuse to examine updated information that could deepen our understanding. We resist the new and cling to the old, which is how people stay stuck in the same mindset. Real growth occurs when we accept the truth by recognizing when our outdated views are no longer relevant.

Biases impact the way we judge ourselves, others, ideas, and situations. As seen in the above scenario, when we're driven by ego, we may think we're more capable than we are.

If you find yourself tending toward feeding your ego, take a step back. Be skeptical and ask yourself if you're really ready to take on the challenge, or whether there's more work for you to do. The truth is, you can do anything you put your mind to—even become a world champion—but the journey is likely to be long and require patience. There's no need to rush; that will only set you back.

We are not always reliable narrators when it comes to our own lives. To grow, we must take notice of the mechanisms quietly shaping our thoughts in the background. In Bryan's case, he might have listened to his coach's advice to help him strategize more effectively during his fights.

Look at situations from multiple angles beyond what you already believe. Save yourself the embarrassment of overestimating your abilities.

Key Takeaway

Cognitive Biases are like invisible puppet strings if we aren't aware of them and let them take control.

Know thy enemy

Biased thinking disrupts your thinking by causing you to miss perspectives that may be more rational than your own.

There are a few major biases that sabotage our critical thinking and self-perception. We must become aware of them, so we can see the logical fallacies we may otherwise fall prey to. Being aware of these biases will allow us to utilize skeptical thinking to recognize when this is happening and break free from the bias.

Cognitive bias 1: Holding yourself to a different standard than others

Consider this:

Shane's friend gets into a car accident because they were texting while driving. It costs them $2,500 in repairs. Shane judges them harshly, calling them stupid. Yet, the same thing happened to him months earlier, making his reaction the height of hypocrisy.

Do you see how Shane's bias blinded him to his own faults in this situation?

By being skeptical about our thoughts, we can see the situation more objectively and help others who have made the same mistakes we have in the past. If this happened to us, rather than being hypocritical and laughing at our friend's misfortune, we could be humble and offer advice based on our experience, acknowledging that texting while driving is dangerous.

We're all on an even playing field, and we shouldn't judge people for not living up to standards we can't meet ourselves.

Cognitive bias 2: Sunk cost fallacy

Consider this:

> Alexa has been dating someone for two years, but the love is gone. The relationship has grown stale, yet Alexa holds on out of comfort or an inability to accept that it's over. She convinces herself that nothing is wrong, but deep down, she's unhappy and feels stuck.

A skeptical thinker would examine what life could look like without the relationship rather than staying out of bias. People fear change, and it's also tempting to continue doing something we've invested a lot into, even if we're not getting anything out of it. Sometimes it seems easier to remain stuck with no room for growth. As an aside, this is also how people lose thousands of dollars gambling, but in other cases, it can lead to opportunity costs.

Sunk cost biases blind us to our flawed thinking. The treatment is to engage our skepticism and evaluate the situation from all angles so we can challenge our biases and change our opinion if need be.

How to recognize biases in real time

Catching ourselves in the act can be difficult. While it is much easier to reflect on what should have happened after a situation is over, sometimes we must react in the moment.

If you happen to catch yourself mid-bias, pause. Interrupt the pattern and think about the other person's perspective. Being reactive doesn't just mean getting aggressive and emotional; it can also be positive, referring to staying calm and figuring out the situation you are currently dealing with.

Real-time awareness helps prevent poor decisions, most notably in high-pressure environments or escalating conflicts. Catching ourselves in the act is very disruptive; we suddenly realize we don't have all the facts and are approaching the situation with one-dimensional thinking.

In an emergency, thinking quickly will not only minimize risk but could potentially save lives. It's even better when we have other people to team up with, as it means we can combine all biased perspectives to get closer to the truth.

If we start working with humility, we can see whether we are being impacted by bias. If we find ourselves in a conversation that is going nowhere, having the humility to recognize that we are falling into our biases means we can start fixing our faults so we can determine who actually lacks knowledge on the conversation topic. It might be us, or it may be the other person. If we lack the knowledge, it's important to be humble and respect that the other person knows what they're talking about.

Being proven wrong is an opportunity to learn something new. Everyone's level of knowledge is different. We all have different beliefs and views. Some are factual, some are theories that may be accurate, and some are flat-out irrational. When we challenge others or are challenged ourselves, it's essential to be humble. Humility helps us avoid being clouded by bias, especially when we are proven wrong. The humble approach prevents embarrassment.

Recognizing bias is about developing the internal sensitivity to catch ourselves when we notice we are drifting into false comfort or lazy thinking. Over time, we'll become better at considering all angles to find the best results.

Replacing bias with better thinking habits

Rewiring the mind to replace bias takes patience and discipline, but it's a process we become better at over time. The more we practice and learn from mistakes, the more intelligent we become. We develop a healthy level of skepticism, cultivate better thinking habits, so we remain open to new views, find our faults, and adjust our opinions when our reasoning leads us to more accurate answers.

The fact is, we can't remove all bias. Some beliefs are so firmly embedded that we accept them as facts. Society views a certain solution as the most accurate, and we stand by that answer.

Other biases may have been proven wrong, yet we still hold onto them, and that's okay. The brain needs to be trained to think more clearly over time, and our perception will shift gradually. Good things take time, so it's important not to be hard on ourselves; the truth will eventually set us free.

If we expose ourselves to diverse perspectives and remain open to these ideas, we can begin to shift our identities from someone who's usually right to someone who improves their thinking. This can only be a very positive thing.

Being skeptical of our own biases allows us to accept when someone challenges something we say. Not everyone is right all the time. All the great thinkers throughout history have been wrong at one time or another. No one is perfect.

Challenging biased thinking patterns demonstrates maturity, which develops over time and enhances the thrill we feel during engaging discussions. Remember, skepticism doesn't mean doubting everything; it signifies respecting the truth enough to question your own mind, thereby fostering greater intelligence. Bias won't be entirely eradicated; instead, skepticism helps you grow beyond bias's control.

Try This Now

Think of something that you believe to be 'right' and question it. Be skeptical. Challenge yourself to improve how you think about it. Work through your biased thinking patterns one by one, identifying and challenging each one.

Go Deeper

In a discussion, invite others to challenge your views in a debate format rather than through a heated argument. Open your mind to see another person's perspective and evaluate whether their sources are more credible than your own.

Remember This

Question your own opinions respectfully to discover what is actually true.

Avoid Emotional Manipulation

Jake is the owner of a small business with five employees. One of his employees, Paul, is always telling Jake how well the business is run and that Jake is the most competent manager he's ever worked for. Jake appreciates the compliments, particularly when he is doubting himself and the future of his business; being a small business owner is difficult, and it's nice to know that someone thinks he's on the right track.

When it comes time to divide responsibilities, Paul suggests that he would be a good fit for more front-of-house work and customer liaison. Jake doesn't hesitate and places Paul in that position immediately, without considering his other employees and their skills. After all, Paul has always been highly supportive of what Jake is trying to achieve.

It doesn't take long before Jake starts losing clients. When he digs deeper, he discovers that they've lost trust in the company through Paul's attitude and inability to work as a leader with clients one-on-one. Too late, Jake realizes that he should not have allowed Paul to inflate his ego to the point that he was blind to the individual skillsets of his employees.

People may manipulate you in different ways—guilt-tripping or flattering you so you will overlook their inadequacies or blind you to their true motives. In Jake's case above, Paul used compliments to get favorable treatment, despite not being very good at his job. Jake's inability to see through this emotional manipulation led to him losing clients and potentially losing skilled employees because he'd overlooked them for leadership roles.

Skepticism is the practice of questioning assumptions, evaluating evidence, and holding back judgment until sufficient evidence is available. Skeptics aren't cynical; they maintain a healthy doubt towards claims while remaining open to being proven wrong when presented with irrefutable evidence.

Skeptics know when someone is manipulating them; they can smell bullshit from a mile away. They'll counter emotional manipulation by pausing, questioning, and even walking away to assess whether someone has nefarious intentions. The skeptic remains cautious when someone's actions, words, or body language suggest negative motives. They remain observant until they get a clear answer to their concerns.

How are skepticism and emotional manipulation linked?

Knowing what we now do about skepticism, we can delve into emotional manipulation through the eyes of a skeptic. Emotional manipulation occurs when people use controlling language to elicit particular feelings for their own benefit. The manipulator wants something from their mark, and it's typically for the mark to make a decision that hurts them but helps the manipulator. The mark rarely gains anything; they only lose energy.

To escape emotional manipulation, develop emotional awareness so you don't fall into traps set by fear, guilt, or flattery. Each time you recognize manipulation, you become more intelligent and build greater self-trust.

But don't rush into cynicism unless the other person is so obviously manipulative that alarm bells start ringing. Skepticism is a protective tool for maintaining healthy doubt about someone's behavior. Too much skepticism is only paranoia, and that isn't healthy.

Key Takeaway

Understanding what emotional manipulation is and being aware of it is key to growth.

Emotional awareness before judgment

You can train your inner skeptic to build your awareness.

Some people are so cynical that they disapprove of others before giving them due consideration; their intentions might seem bad from their perspective, but maybe they just misread them.

On the opposite side of the spectrum, others are so gullible that they fall for manipulation instantly, becoming completely submissive to the manipulator.

Our emotional responses aren't inherently bad, but it's important to try to keep a clear head when examining someone's intentions, especially in critical situations. We should be cautious of manipulators' actions and not base our judgment solely on our emotional responses. That's how manipulators get us; when emotion overwhelms our logic, and we can't find a state of calm, we've fallen straight into the manipulator's grasp.

To avoid being drawn into the manipulator's world, it is crucial that we become more aware of our emotional states. What triggers and weak points do we need to work on? Do we fear easily? Are we easily guilt-tripped and find ourselves worrying too much about others? Are we weak to flattery because it feeds our ego?

How to avoid emotional manipulation

There are a few things we can do to start working toward being able to avoid falling victim to emotional manipulation:

- Figure out what your indulgences are, as these can be your downfall.
- Train yourself to strengthen these weak points so you can always stay a few steps ahead of the manipulator—it's like a game of chess.

It's a cruel world out there. There are master manipulators who are so committed to the game that they'll literally marry you to control you and take over. They make manipulation their full-time occupation as con-artists. I hope you never run into anyone like this.

Awareness helps get us out of trouble by making us better at spotting people's bad intentions. Awareness also forces us to recognize that there is evil out there.

However, it is important that we don't use these manipulative tactics ourselves. Instead, we should focus on just recognizing when others are using them so we don't fall for them.

Being controlled by a manipulator can change the course of a person's life. It might be a loved one with attachment issues who controls a family member for their own comfort, preventing them from being independent. While they are unaware, we recognize that this is selfish behavior.

Emotional awareness that conquers manipulation helps us become more mature and better decision-makers.

Sometimes maturity means making tough decisions we know are right, like cutting off a close friend who is holding us back in life. It may be that they are trying to manipulate people into staying stagnant with them, rather than moving forward. It's a bold move that requires courage, but the mature thing to do is let this 'friendship' go so you can elevate yourself.

Spotting Red Flags

When we can detect the emotional traps manipulators set, we can avoid them. Being aware of these traps brings a sense of calm. People will respect the way we work the room. Just by being quiet and observing the 'snakes' in the room, the snakes in turn will become aware of us, and won't want to mess around. In fact, they'll see that they can't, so they'll choose not to.

Manipulators will fear us, even without much action on our part.

Here are some practical methods skeptical thinkers use to identify and resist emotional traps:

Don't rush decisions

Think before you act. Rushing means losing yourself in the moment, which you can't afford when your reputation is on the line. Be observant of others' actions. If someone becomes aggressive, don't reveal your triggers—walk away and assess skeptically why they're being reactive. If you rush, you're liable to end up in a fistfight and tarnish your reputation.

Question excessive flattery

You don't need validation from someone who is targeting your insecurities and flattering you for personal gain. Build confidence in yourself. If you share too much, people will use your weak points to control you. Accept yourself, then think skeptically about how others try to gain control by recognizing the red flags you've avoided.

Gather evidence

Find out who is emotionally manipulating you, what their intentions are, and whether they have a healthy or dark history. Verify your sources and question their motives. Determine whether they're genuine or whether they're only trying to get something from you.

Thoughtful questioning like this is not paranoia. It's a healthy thinking pattern that helps you communicate strategically. You never know when you need to be cautious with someone—they could be attempting to manipulate you to control your life, finances, or career. This caution pays off when they show their true colors. And if you end up being wrong, that's fine too! No one is right all the time, and no harm was done.

Keep challenging emotionally manipulative techniques in everyday life, so you know when to pick your battles, especially when someone is targeting your livelihood with manipulation tactics.

From victim to master – building a skeptical mindset for lifelong growth

Many people are easy to read if you think clearly about their intentions; however, skepticism is a daily practice, not just a defensive response. Identifying the 'master' manipulators takes practice.

Manipulators take so much energy from us when we fall for their empty words and actions. It is tiring and wastes time and energy we could be using to work on ourselves. Using skeptical thinking to question people's intentions means we can walk away from a situation before it gets out of hand.

What if you're wrong?

If your skepticism is proven wrong, embrace it rather than getting upset. Sometimes you want to be proven wrong. If you suspect a loved one is attempting to manipulate you, but it turns out they only had pure intentions, that's a big relief. Skepticism is not about being a cynic, after all, so being wrong is a good thing. It means you're in good company.

Being a skeptic encourages lifelong learning. It helps you become a free thinker with an independent mindset. You can be the type of person who entertains someone else's point of view, even if you don't fully buy into it due to a lack of evidence. That's the beauty of being open to changing your views.

Skepticism helps us in all aspects of our lives—with our relationships, business, and personal goals. Getting too emotional around other people will only stress us out and put us in a negative state of mind. Skeptical thinking helps us pursue the truth in a healthy way while remaining open to being proven wrong.

I personally believe it's a brilliant way to think, especially when you are very biased and never challenge your deeply-held beliefs. That's the beauty of life; when others challenge your perspective and end up proving you wrong, you learn something. Rather than being emotional and holding onto an opinion that no longer serves you, you can move on from it and grow. In fact, when you are proven wrong, you should become more confident, not less.

As a master skeptic, the point is to be proven wrong. Humbly accepting when you're wrong is a healthy way to be.

Try This Now

Analyze people you come across today and work on distinguishing between the genuine people and the conniving ones. Start with the blatant manipulators and work up to identifying the signs of the 'master manipulators'.

Go Deeper

Question your own and other people's situations when they are being manipulated. Offer to help others out. By helping others, you are also helping yourself grow your mindset.

Remember This

We become masters of skepticism through failure. Even if we do end up being manipulated, that unpleasant experience is an opportunity to learn from our mistakes and employ our skeptical mindset to avoid the next manipulator.

Stay Open to Changing Your Mind

Carolyn has an online store where she sells original handmade clothes. Her sales are solid, and she has a growing client base. Recently, she received some feedback from a colleague, who noted a couple of flaws in a recent design and she suggested a workaround that she believed could potentially boost sales.

Carolyn had never received negative feedback about any of her creations and, as sales were good, firmly disagreed with her colleague's opinion and decided to ignore her advice. Over time, sales on this product slowed down in comparison to other products, and Carolyn realized her colleague's suggestion would have elevated the design—she just couldn't see it.

Updating your beliefs when you encounter new evidence may seem discouraging to some people, and many of us are not willing to do this. However, think of it like this: discovering new insights and taking them on board can be both intriguing and essential for professional and personal growth.

Whenever we're proven wrong, our instinct is to be stubborn and not accept new truths. This internal resistance is something we all face when confronting evidence that contradicts beliefs we've held for a long time, particularly if we've defended these beliefs for years and built our identity around them. We can easily become emotionally attached to our beliefs because they bring us comfort.

Even after being shown discrediting evidence, people often cling to their original beliefs. We persevere because we can't accept what has been presented to us. Some of us struggle with new truths and remain stuck in our old ways, which hold us back when those beliefs play a significant role in our lives. This dampens our ability to see other possibilities. Acceptance is the right approach when old beliefs have been superseded by new understanding.

If a commitment to a belief is so strong that we are unwilling to consider it may be wrong, it's understandable that we wouldn't want to let it go. However, having an open mind when we are confronted with good evidence that contradicts what we believe may be difficult, but accepting change prevents our thinking from becoming outdated. Life evolves. We learn from old ways and develop better solutions.

Key Takeaway

If you want to see change in your free thinking, break down these stubborn psychological barriers of bias so you can open your mind to new ways, beliefs, and knowledge.

The power of evidence and intellectual honesty

Evidence plays a crucial role in skeptical thinking and uncovering the truth. If we're lazy and only look half-heartedly into evidence without enthusiasm, we won't perceive what is credible. We need to have a genuine interest in getting to the truth.

Good evidence comes from reliable sources with proven facts. It could be from a professional in a field of work who has tested their hypothesis and has become a proven, credible source. They provide evidence to the world through various methods, including written documentation, video recordings, and audio recordings. We analyze this material with healthy doubt to assess the intellectual honesty of what intelligent professionals have presented, especially when their work has been peer-reviewed by other experts who have judged the evidence to be factual. The more people who recognize truth in an analysis, the stronger our belief becomes, even if we were initially biased toward an opposing view. The evidence allows us to adopt the new belief with an open mind.

Intellectual honesty means being reasonable with yourself. It's a skeptic's guiding principle: value truth over comfort. Comfort doesn't change the fact that truth is truth, whether you like it or not. Comfort simply means clinging to one-dimensional thinking rather than accepting the new and leaving behind the outdated.

Have the maturity to examine firm evidence and be willing to update your beliefs to become more intelligent. Always value truth, even when it hurts. Skeptical thinking isn't for everyone—it can be overwhelming, especially regarding deeply held beliefs. But for everyday use, it's a practical way to find the best solution by healthily doubting some claims and agreeing with the most accurate ones.

Skeptical thinking means we're always open to being proven wrong because our allegiance is to evidence, not our beliefs. Influential skeptics aren't negative or cynical—they are open-minded. They adopt the beliefs that are supported by the most credible evidence and accept anyone's challenge to prove them wrong.

I don't see healthy-minded skeptics as negative doubters. I see them as having the intellectual maturity to stand with the facts until proven otherwise.

Practical techniques for staying open-minded

Staying open-minded allows us to elevate our inner skeptic. If we learn to enjoy it when someone challenges our beliefs, especially when the topic is something of great interest to us, we're testing our ability to find answers, even if we end up being proven wrong. In addition, the topics we discuss don't need to be ones we are personally invested in; they can be about anything we see substance in.

Technique #1: Question yourself

Start with "What evidence would change my mind?" This prompts deep introspection and helps you consider another point of view. Even if your evidence is solid, taking someone else's points into account may reveal a breakthrough concept that elevates your belief. A single piece of strong evidence could be a game-changer. Identify inconsistencies in your own logic—this analysis deepens your understanding and may provide insights for a new direction. Question yourself as much as you question others' beliefs, and update your views when it becomes necessary.

Technique #2: Learn from other skeptics

Listen to competent skeptics on podcasts to see how they articulate their beliefs, remain open to challenges, and accept being proven wrong. Observe intelligent debaters online and note their confidence in presenting their points, their openness to discussion, and their willingness to engage with the most credible evidence while awaiting correction. Read their content in books, articles, and magazines. Research how their skeptical minds work. Perfecting these skills may help you elevate your own thinking. This is how free thinkers remain independent in their minds despite the challenges they may face.

Technique #3: Learn from disagreement

Initially, you may become emotional when you disagree with something, but with maturity, these disagreements transform from heated arguments into respectful and truth-seeking conversations, where the goal is to get to the facts.

When discussing serious topics, maintain professionalism. This demonstrates maturity and encourages the other person to respond respectfully while you work together to uncover the truth behind the belief.

The benefits of changing your mind

Changing our minds when encountering new evidence is far from a sign of weakness. It gives us credibility. It's the starting point for personal growth, clarity, and wisdom. To accept new evidence takes courage; it does not denote weakness. No one is right all the time, and today's evidence may be superseded by something else tomorrow. Logic can change when it is challenged by someone who puts in the hard work to make the change.

Skepticism brings out brilliance. When we look into the evidence, we begin to recognize how much complexity our minds can handle. Each time we seek evidence with an open mind and allow our beliefs to be challenged, we sharpen our thinking. An active mind never stops learning—it continues growing into that of an intelligent free thinker.

Even uncertainty can be beneficial, preventing one-dimensional thinking and potentially leading to breakthroughs that achieve a high level of certainty in topics few people understand. If we can provide this information and teach others, updating everyone with new hypotheses backed by credible sources, we'll gain respect from professionals, enthusiasts, and amateurs alike. Reputations are built through courageous acts of finding truth, even when that means updating our own beliefs.

Throughout history, changed minds have changed industries, societies, and relationships. Consider the food industry, where low-fat foods were pushed as a healthier option. Consumers accepted this uncritically, buying these products without questioning the credibility of the claim.

Conversely, professionals in the industry, like nutritionists and scientists, engaged their skepticism by questioning why people consuming these low-fat products weren't getting healthier. This necessitated further research, which revealed that low-fat products were packed with sugars and additives for better taste—but they were worse for health. They made the public aware through skeptical statements that not all fats are bad, and the sugars added to these products were the real problem.

By proving their hypothesis, the experts changed their own minds and those of the public. While they may have initially believed the claim, observations led them to ask questions, find evidence, and solve the problem.

Try This Now

Consider a belief you have held for a long time. Decide if you still resonate with it. If not (or even if you do), start looking at a different point of view to elevate the belief.

Go Deeper

Strive to reach insights that update your beliefs. Your goal is to reach a certain level of clarity, which then heightens your intellect.

Remember This

By remaining open to changing your mind, you remain open to new evidence.

Principle 4 Recap:

Question Authority (the Right Way)

Core Idea 1: Bias blinds growth — when you assume you're right, you stop learning.

Core Idea 2: Skepticism is strength — questioning yourself protects you from manipulation and false certainty.

Core Idea 3: Truth evolves — the wise update their beliefs when better evidence appears.

One-liner reminder: "Respect truth enough to question your own mind."

Free Thinker Exercise Box

- ▹ **Bias Check-In:** Catch one bias today. Ask: "What evidence would actually change my mind?"
- ▹ **Pause & Reframe:** When emotions rise, pause 10 seconds. Then ask: "What else could be true?"
- ▹ **Manipulation Radar:** When flattered or guilt-tripped, quietly ask: "Who benefits if I agree?"
- ▹ **Belief Audit:** Pick one long-held belief. Research three credible sources that disagree and see what shifts.

Goal: Build the humility to challenge your own thinking, stay alert to emotional traps, and evolve with new evidence.

Free Thinker Challenge (Optional)

For the next 48 hours, preface your strongest opinions with "I might be wrong, but..." Notice how this simple phrase opens your mind and earns respect from others who value truth over ego.

Principle 5:
Challenge Cultural Norms

"Be the change you wish to see happen."

— Arleen Lorrance

The fifth of the seven principles of Free Thinking is where independence extends beyond institutions and into social identity. Leadership, magnetism, and dropping ego help you see culture not as truth, but as influence.

This principle develops the confidence to stand apart without needing validation or dominance.

7 Principles of Free Thinking

Claim Your Beliefs

Curiosity Without Fear

Listen Deeper Speak Smarter

Question Authority

Write Your Own Script

Pursue the Unconventional Path

Leadership

Joe is leading a company with ten employees. His overarching goal is to build an empire, but for now, he wants to innovate on a new product to propel his business forward.

As a leader, Joe knows he needs his employees to see his vision. Rather than commanding through dictatorial control, Joe pitches his idea and, in doing so, earns the respect of his employees. They confirm, through their words and actions, that they believe in Joe's work and can see his vision. They indicate their readiness to help him build it.

Leadership is not for the faint of heart. Many people believe they are not suited to leadership; however, it's essential to recognize that leadership is a rewarding journey toward building the empire we envisioned from the start.

It begins when we ask ourselves, "What if?" and envision turning an original idea into reality. Leadership skills are critical to making this happen.

Leadership in the creative sector is truly envisioning a future that does not yet exist and convincing others to rally towards it. As with Joe's case above, it may be your vision, but your employees are the ones who must build it. Influential leaders are talented storytellers who win others over to their vision, inventing possibilities that inspire innovative pursuits. These new ways of thinking draw people to believe in our ideas.

Imagination is one of the most important leadership tools. If we happen to be the key person on a project, it is up to us to develop the main ideas, listen to others' input, and use our imagination to synthesize all the concepts into a solution for accomplishing the project. Imagination allows the vision to flow, showing our team a picture they can create in their minds.

Creativity in leadership isn't artistic fluff or wasted time—it's strategic thinking that drives innovation and growth. Many companies today highly value employees who think creatively on their own, which means leaders must do the same. Creative thinking is crucial for leaders, employees, and company environments seeking innovation.

Key Takeaway

Leadership is all about innovative thinking and inspiring others in new ways.

Innovation is the compass of leadership

To true leaders of a specific field, innovation doesn't just mean progress—it means reshaping the whole playing field. Progress matters, but transforming the industry changes the entire game, leading the company in a direction that will be written in the history books. People centuries from now will remember this accomplishment.

When it comes to leadership, innovation is our compass. With our creative thinking, we can create paths to unimaginable heights. True leaders embrace the unknown.

The connection between creative thinking and innovation is powerful. To innovate, we must think creatively to solve problems others ignore. Ignoring issues can be damaging, even catastrophic. It's like taking shortcuts, and that's not okay when we're trying to create something new for a company, product, or art style. Leaders think creatively to solve these problems with grit as they strive to achieve the best results.

When the work becomes tedious, difficult, and repetitive, this connection between creative thinking and innovation is even more necessary. It takes determination and resolve to continue thinking creatively about the problems others don't want to solve.

Innovation requires risk-taking, especially when people experiment with ideas no one has seen or done before. Breaking old, venerable systems takes courage, but if you succeed, the reward can be astronomical. Using innovation as our compass not only makes things interesting and worthwhile, but it leads to risky breakthroughs—a difficult and exciting venture that makes you feel alive if you have the guts to follow through.

Do you have what it takes for a risk-reward venture?

Let's say it again: innovation is the compass born from creative thinking, and it's a necessary system we must follow.

Empowering others to create

If we want to create, we must have a team that we empower. Creative leadership doesn't mean controlling all the original ideas; it means inspiring others to think for themselves. A great leader connects with their team, unlocking creativity in others by showing an immense passion for the project. This motivates the team to think creatively and offer insights that enhance concepts and solutions.

If we want to excel with our concepts, we can't be stubborn. There's always room for improvement. Once we set aside ego, we can use our teams wisely. When we motivate them to think creatively, they may develop something that enhances our original idea. And when that happens, we'll be grateful we used our team effectively.

Seeking opinions from people who think similarly to us in our field is always beneficial, and this is what collaborative, idea-driven leadership looks like. With our idea as the foundation, we can then work with our team build on it and reach the desired result. Using the traditional leadership model, where we simply command everyone to adopt our biased perspective, will lead to our team lacking enthusiasm and motivation.

Hot tip: Stay energetic and ensure everyone is involved.

Team effort with multiple minds at work always enhances solutions. In all cases, solutions come quicker and with less stress than when we are working alone. It's simple—great leaders always choose to empower others to achieve the best results.

Create a culture where everyone feels safe to speak up about their creative ideas and take risks. As leaders, we can build a focused, driven culture with a positive atmosphere, giving others the confidence to contribute their creativity. When we make the environment worthwhile for others, people will view their work not just as a job, but as a career where they can grow.

Being a fair leader earns you the respect you deserve. Empowering others creates significant progress on your road to success.

This journey doesn't have to be solitary. It is always beneficial to have a helping hand, no matter what industry you are in. You should also be compassionate as you build others up around you.

Vision, courage, and the creative legacy

Vision and courage separate mediocre leaders from great ones. Leaders with creativity are known for their bold vision. The unknown frightens many people, but great leaders navigate uncertainty. They accept that in the unknown, anything is possible—good or bad—and consider it worth pursuing.

Great leaders focus on vision while practicing delayed gratification. They take steps toward success one day at a time. Their vision provides them with a long-term idea that guides daily work and leads the team in that direction, showing them a path toward success. Leaders with a clear vision for transforming an industry know that assembling a team and getting them on board with the vision are actions they need to prepare for. A powerful vision must be the first step in forming a concept because, without this vision, we will struggle to take the risks necessary to innovate.

Courage diminishes fear. With an unclear future born from the unknown, a bold leader must have the resilience to push through at all costs. There's no point in fearing the worst-case scenario when the best results are also possible. Bravery is a characteristic anyone can learn, but most cannot handle. My advice is to set a higher standard for your pain threshold, so you worry less and pursue the outcome you desire. Never doubt yourself—the world will do that for you. Doubt is the poison of success and leads to failure.

Be courageous enough to ignore the naysayers and keep focused on the goal you've worked hard to envision. Unique ideas cause people to misunderstand creative leaders. But when others don't see how a vision is possible, great leaders don't feel discouraged or give up—they persevere.

Leaders must first lead themselves with kindness, confidence, and consistent learning. They're good to themselves even when others don't see eye to eye with their perspectives; that's how leaders keep their heads above water and never sink. That's how they lead the worthwhile life they've always dreamed of.

Try This Now

Ask yourself what your life's work is. Jot down what you need to achieve it. Create a plan so the idea has structure, which gets you a step closer to your purpose.

Go Deeper

Start focusing on your goals with actions. Work on it day to day and persevere all the way until the end, no matter how long it takes.

Remember This

Always trust your instincts, even if they direct you on a long and difficult journey.

Magnetism

Despite having the same upbringing, siblings Kim and Toby could not be more dissimilar. Where Toby struggles to draw people to him to follow his creative work as an artist, Kim has no difficulty gaining followers for her creative practice. It's not that Toby is not talented; he absolutely is, but he just doesn't seem able to attract the same interest his sister does.

Kim wanted to help Toby, so she engaged a professional to audit their social media pages. Among minor changes in branding and consistency, the professional noted a considerable difference in confidence. Kim was happy to put herself out there, not caring what others thought. She was happy to be herself—like it or leave it. Toby, on the other hand, was much more reserved. He didn't want to be seen as 'silly' or 'full of himself', but this stopped him from being his true engaging self.

Once Toby understood this and was brave enough to post about himself in an open, honest way, his followers—and commissions—began to soar.

Magnetism plays a big part in being influential. I like to say magnetism is about being our true selves. Not everyone will like or understand our unique ways, but we are not here to please the entire world.

The thing is, even if we don't stand out and attract others, someone will still dislike us. We can choose to be our authentic selves and attract people naturally with the power of magnetism, or we can blend into the crowd. It's a choice only we can make.

We won't be flirting with love interests all the time, after all. In a crowd, we radiate a visible presence as someone who doesn't conform but stays true to their character. This authenticity is unmatched at events where everyone else follows societal norms. People notice those who stand out, not those who blend in. They're drawn to the uniqueness of someone being themselves. We can spot these people from a mile away; it's so obvious who they are.

When our aura is strong, it attracts the curious while keeping the jealous at a distance (even though they still keep an eye on us). Don't worry about them. Disregard the jealous types and their negative energy; they live in fear of being themselves.

The psychology of attraction has many components. People are drawn to those with creative, original thinking. They respect unique concepts and views, and enjoy learning something new, and seeking inspiration from a rebellious spirit.

When someone seems uninteresting and lacking in personality, we don't ask them for opinions. We're attracted to interesting characters with original perspectives, not people-pleasers who hide in the crowd, afraid to break societal norms.

Stay determined to keep your uplifting spirit strong by always staying true to yourself. If you dare to think differently, the world will notice.

Key Takeaway

Magnetism isn't just about charming others—it's an energetic pull that comes from being our original self.

Be the opposite

Creativity is deeply rooted in creating contrast in a conformist world.

Imagine yourself as a bright color against a grayscale background—you stand out through your unique creative thought while others conform to societal norms. People with magnetism choose the path opposite the herd. While this sounds risky, it can be highly rewarding.

Conforming to the crowd kills magnetism

When we remain within the herd's safe zone, we forfeit the value of standing out. People's minds change quickly. If we lose our magnetism by hiding in the comfort zone of conventional norms, we'll be forgotten. We'll lose our spark and that weird, fun, confident side we love showing the world.

Being bold teaches us to be strict with ourselves. It shows we're not afraid of being misunderstood. Not everyone will understand us, and that's okay. They may question our ideas and perspectives. Conformists with no spark will be our biggest haters and doubters, but boldness teaches us to stay firm in our beliefs.

We should never stop doing our creative work based on the opinions of others. There will always be people who misunderstand us and dislike our unique views, but they are not the enemy. We become our own enemy when we react emotionally to others' opinions and fall into self-doubt.

Stay determined in your actions

Being the opposite makes us influential in many scenarios. Social media is a perfect example. People who stand out from the herd on social media gain millions of followers. Few conformists have the same level of popularity. In meaningful conversations, when a group of eight people follow trending views, and you speak your truth, you stand out—it doesn't matter if you are praised or doubted; the point is that you are unique.

By all means, you should keep standing out by being contrarian, but be careful not to be so outrageous that your views become delusional or irrational. There's a balance. We should avoid being too predictable too, but dare to flip the script when things feel mediocre.

Enjoy being the opposite, show the world your weirdness, and watch how magnetic you will become.

Speak like you believe your thoughts matter

Creative confidence plays an important role in expressing our unique ideas to others. If we believe in our ideas, we need to show the world why they matter. Confidence shows we are enthusiastic and passionate, convincing others to see the vision we see.

A person lacking in confidence will undersell their ideas, which leaves the people they are pitching to uninterested. We must sell our ideas; encourage others to resonate with our point of view.

Magnetic people don't just captivate crowds with unique thoughts but with their conviction. When we hold a belief so strongly that we express it freely with certainty, others think, "Wow, those ideas actually make sense!" Because we're so confident in our belief, we win others over.

However, we won't achieve this without fleshing out our ideas and showing how they work in practice. It's important to back up our ideas with detail and conviction so we can express them with confidence.

The biggest block to creative magnetism is trying to be liked.

Judgment is part of life. People will constantly judge us. They will tell us our ideas won't work, and may even say we're crazy.

Don't let yourself become discouraged. Let them judge. Your perseverance will keep them watching, and, over time, more people will pay attention—and that's magnetism. Yes, it also attracts negativity, but don't fear it. If we're confident in our beliefs, it won't matter. When our ideas work out, we'll prove the detractors wrong and gain more confidence.

Be the creative thinker who shows such passion in your work that confidence radiates off you naturally.

Speak from the soul and not from a script. Practice so you can flow naturally with your ideas, rather than sitting there in awkwardness or fumbling over your words. Experience the magic of the work that was created. Maintain your confidence constantly, not just momentarily.

Become a source of energy, not noise

Being a positive source of energy, turning sour moods into uplifting ones not only helps us but also helps others.

When we uplift someone—not just to share an idea but by being decent—we can make their day or even change their life. Magnetic people inspire others and challenge them to grow, providing value in a way that benefits everyone. People may not express it outright, but they will appreciate you continuing to be a light of positive energy, especially when there is darkness all around.

It doesn't matter; we do not quit.

Be mindful of the difference between attention-seeking noise and the powerful, energetic force that provides value. If we seek attention with ideas lacking meaning, we won't gain respect, and people won't want to be around that dull energy.

Never act with malicious intentions or false urgency. Be someone who shines in every room. People will come up to you wanting to know something about you that they don't yet understand, but would like to find out. Energy is everything.

Creative thinkers don't win others over by being selfish—instead, they're selfless, solution-oriented, and always willing to help other people. They're serious but can be playful, adding joy to the mix. They don't overthink things, which means they don't fall into worry. This form of magnetism creates a strong energetic pull because these people provide value with a work-hard attitude while maintaining an equally strong play-hard attitude.

Magnetic people focus on others' emotional tone, sensing their vibe. They project enthusiastic energy while recognizing emotions in others and themselves. It's not just intellectual; connecting through ideas involves emotions and substance.

A magnetic person helps others feel more alive. This is why people prefer them over those who conform and act selfishly.

Try This Now

On a day when your energy is high vibration, go and spread positivity to the people around you just by being your happy self.

Go Deeper

Now see how many of the people around you are drawn to your vibe. Maybe they are coming closer and speaking to you. Use your high-energy days wisely to project your positivity onto others.

Remember This

Be the character who provides that special gift by valuing others, uplifting them, and walking away from your conversation feeling a little extra touch of life.

Drop Ego

Roman emperor Marcus Aurelius was a Stoic philosopher and the most powerful person in the Roman Empire at one time. In public, everyone would bow down to him, show him respect, and follow his commands.

When he walked through town, people showered him with praise, treating him like a saviour. This man was one of the most influential individuals of the time. Yet he hired a servant to accompany him as he visited prominent locations to whisper in his ear: "You're just a man."

Remember this: You are not better than anyone!

No one is better than you, either.

Basically, it's time we all started treating everyone as equals. It's the truth. We all bleed, breathe, and think. We are all human.

There's this made-up food chain where more prominent, powerful, and financially wealthy people look down on "Average Joes" and the less fortunate. Not all may say it, but their actions tell the story.

Once you reach high levels of success, please don't be like these people. They need to learn humility. It is not only the narcissistic megalomaniacs, obviously. Some people run the streets engaging in criminal activity, gain a reputation for seeing themselves as superior to others, and mistreat lost people in society.

It is bizarre for someone to think they are actually better than others. We can free ourselves from the need to be superior by recognizing that we're all on different levels in our lives. First step: finding our true selves. Stop competing with others to get one up on them. When we see someone doing well, and we're not at that level yet, we may become bitter and jealous, praying for their downfall. When they face adversity, we see an opportunity to take them down—in business, relationships, appearance, or any arena. This is pure ego-driven behavior, and it's evil. That's not who we are!

There is nothing wrong with competition, but we have to see it as us against ourselves. We need to remain focused on our goal without looking in the direction of others. We can't get caught up thinking about how we want to destroy them. We are in our lane, and they are in theirs. It's great to come out the winner, but when we are using dirty, unethical tactics for personal gain, it'll come back to hurt us one day.

As someone who has used these dirty tactics, I learned that the hard way. It's great being at the top—but it doesn't last forever.

Approach competition in a focused, driven, and humble way. We can still reach our goals and win—we'll just stress less, avoid destructive anger, and find the journey more meaningful. It's the decent thing to do.

If we are in a management position, it's best to avoid seeing ourselves as better than those below us. We're simply more experienced because of the hard work we've put in. Anyone who works hard can reach our position or higher. Times change, and young people entering industries eventually take over.

Key Takeaway

Being at the top doesn't last forever; it's more important to stay humble and free ourselves from our egos.

Listen more, speak less

The loudest voice in the room is the weakest.

Some people try to be the star of every conversation, over-energetic and don't deign to listen to others because they think they're too important to hear what others have to say. They speak over people, act cocky, and assume they're always right when they could actually be wrong and miss a valuable learning experience. Most people can't stand this behavior.

If you speak less and listen more, you'll be a far better conversation partner, and you'll learn more.

Listening to others means gaining their perspective and understanding their point of view. Listening is the best communication skill—it teaches you how someone truly thinks and feels. If you're perceptive and pay attention, you can figure people out: their strengths, weaknesses, and habits. When you listen, people feel important. Many people can also be quite open. They find it hard to keep quiet about important parts of their lives, though you need to be a certain type of person to get these secrets out of others. They open up to you, gaining trust and comfort, which builds respect.

Unfortunately, some use these tactics for manipulation and personal gain. But those who listen with empathy and genuine care can help change lives. Listening more than you speak allows you to resonate with others and treat them as equals. Practical thinkers will use their valuable skill of listening more than they speak to connect with others, placing them not first, not last, but right beside you.

Silence is a power in itself. People don't need to know what you're thinking all the time. Speak when you have valuable input. Let others talk so you can observe and discern who is genuine and who is deceitful. Listening is both a tool for dropping ego and working with humility, and a way to stay cautious.

Keep your ears open, speak when you have something valuable to say, and keep observing.

You're just a man

Reread the story from the start of this chapter. Think about it for a second: Roman emperor Marcus Aurelius really offered a powerful lesson in humility and dropping ego.

He was the most powerful man in the empire. He could have whatever he wanted. Yet, he had a servant—levels below his status—remind him that he was no different from anyone else. Aurelius himself instructed the servant to do this.

Fascinating, right?

Imagine if more people in positions of power remembered who they actually were: mere humans! No better than the servant whispering those words.

This reminder kept Aurelius grounded and his ego in check. While other Roman emperors thrived on ego and are remembered for their cruelty, Marcus is remembered as one of history's most influential figures because of his humility. He had the foresight to constantly remind himself to be humble so he wouldn't lose self-control amid constant praise. With immense pressure and people constantly telling him how good and amazing he was, it would have been easy to believe he was truly better than everyone else and start looking down on people.

This is how we lose ourselves: by abusing our power and behaving as if we are above everyone else.

When we lose self-control and perspective, we believe we're invincible and can do whatever we want. This is why people in positions of power—no matter their status—must drop their ego and work with humility. We never know when our empire may crumble.

Never think you're better than anyone.

Free yourself from pride and social status

Let go of the false identity you've given yourself.

Recognize reality for what it is: we're all equals.

Service others to service yourself.

Don't play manipulative games with malicious intent for personal gain.

Thinking of yourself as more than you are leads to an obsession with pride and a need to prove your worth to others. This makes people miserable. They become beasts, chasing ego boosts to feel validated.

The truth is, we're all individuals, and we all have a need to find our true selves. Once we've done this, we will understand true freedom. The alternative—not accepting ourselves and relying on others to fuel our egos—leads only to emptiness.

When we're completely comfortable with ourselves, we become more successful. In time, we'll earn respect and financial wealth, and we'll start fulfilling our purpose. The alternative—when we gain success through pride—may have people thinking about us for a minute when they hear our name or are in our presence, but once we're out of sight, they don't care at all.

Everyone is busy dealing with their own identity. They don't need to deal with ours as well.

Powerful individuals can attract others who want something from them for their own gain—a bigger position in the organization or a spot on an exclusive board. This can give us an inflated sense of our own importance. To let go is to be aware of our ego: how we act around others, feeling like we always need to be right, comparing ourselves to others, and craving approval.

Our role is not our identity.

A CEO is not always a CEO.

Be a person who serves others without expecting praise or recognition. We know how good our deeds are—we don't need people to worship us or tell the world how fantastic we are.

Let it all go so you can start living as the person you really are.

Try This Now

Tell yourself this: I'm amazing and worthy, just as I am. I don't need anyone's approval. (Tell yourself multiple times, daily, until you believe it.) At the same time, remind yourself that while you are amazing, you are no more amazing than the next person.

Go Deeper

Once you believe that you are amazing, work towards being yourself. Stop masquerading as someone important. Stop trying to impress others. Be you!

Remember This

No level of respect or financial worth has any value if we've gained it through pride.

Principle 5 Recap: **Challenge Cultural Norms**

Core Idea 1: Innovation is leadership — rewrite the default, don't maintain it.

Core Idea 2: Authentic contrast creates magnetism — be the opposite of bland conformity.

Core Idea 3: Humility amplifies impact — drop ego, listen more, and empower others to build with you.

One-liner reminder: "Stand apart without looking down."

Free Thinker Exercise Box

- **The "What-If" Manifesto:** Write a one-page vision that flips a common industry norm. Start with: "What if the rule everyone obeys is wrong?"
- **Opposite Move:** Pick one routine this week (meeting, feature, pitch) and do the smart opposite: shorter, simpler, async, or customer-led.
- **3×3 Empowerment:** Ask three teammates for one bold idea each, then green-light one action per person within 72 hours.
- **Signal > Noise:** In your next meeting, keep a 2:1 listen-to-talk ratio. Summarize others before you weigh in.

- **The Whisper Test:** Before any decision, tell yourself: "You're just a person." Notice how it sharpens judgment and reduces status games.

Goal: Build creative leadership that challenges norms, attracts people through authenticity, and scales by humility.

Free Thinker Challenge (Optional)

24-Hour Prototype & Proof

In one day, prototype a tiny version of your contrarian idea and show it to three users. Ask only:

1. What surprised you?
2. What's missing?
3. Would you use/pay for this today?

From the feedback received, activate the smallest improvement the same week.

Principle 6:

Write Your Own Script

七転び八起き

"Fall down seven times, stand up eight."

— Japanese Proverb

The sixth of the seven principles of Free Thinking turns philosophy into lived experience. Through gratitude, confronting inner demons, and understanding suffering, you learn to shape meaning rather than escape discomfort.

Your life becomes authored, not accidental.

7 Principles of Free Thinking

Claim Your Beliefs

Curiosity Without Fear

Listen Deeper, Speak Smarter

Question Authority

Challenge Cultural Norms

Write Your Own Script

Pursue the Unconventional Path

Gratitude and Appreciation

Aaron was brought up to always say please and thank you, no matter how small the offering or situation was. For this reason, as a child, whenever his mother or father cooked dinner, he always said 'thank you'. His friends thought it was weird, but Aaron considered it completely normal behavior.

As he matured, Aaron began to consider 'why' he was saying thank you. He started to see that the act of cooking dinner wasn't necessarily a small one. Sometimes, his parents were tired after working all day—but they still went to the trouble of preparing something nutritious and delicious. In addition, they also occasionally made an effort to include meals or ingredients their children enjoyed or requested, even when these foods were pricier than the norm or took longer to prepare.

Aaron came to realize that he wasn't just saying 'thank you' for the sake of it but that he was genuinely grateful for his parents' time, care, and effort.

Gratitude is appreciation for what life has given us—the good and the bad, the painful experiences we've worked to overcome, and the joyful times when we felt carefree. It helps us discover why life is worth living, and helps us adjust our mindset so we can see the silver lining even in our darkest moments. Gratitude isn't just a feeling—it's a deliberate act of reflection that can put you in a brighter mood.

Gratitude operates at deeper levels than we often recognize. The gratitude Aaron showed in the scenario above came from a much more meaningful place because there were more emotions involved. As everyday life gets busy, we can fail to appreciate what others have done for us, especially those who were there from the beginning. Reflective thinking helps us find the time and space to understand everything we should be grateful for.

Reflective gratitude requires slowing down to evaluate your life experiences, relationships, and values. We never truly grasp the importance of a moment until we reflect on it later and find we are grateful for being fortunate enough to have experienced it. That's where the true value of gratitude lies: in our darkest moments, gratitude helps us find appreciation for a beautiful moment in time, leading to the realization that life is worth living. And that's when we know everything will be okay.

In our fast-paced, greed-driven society, consumerism and competition over material wealth and social status dull our ability to recognize what we already have. If we have food, water, and shelter, we should be deeply grateful. Many people lack these necessities. Instead of complaining, think about everything you have to be grateful for.

Gratitude can even save your life in the right moment, and, for that reason, I recommend you practice it daily.

Key Takeaway

Gratitude is not just an emotion; it's an inner mirror. It is more about being reflective than reactive.

Invisible gold

Start considering the overlooked riches of everyday life and show appreciation for them more regularly.

Look for the hidden value in ordinary moments. Waking up and commencing our day by looking up at the sky and appreciating the sun's radiance as it beams down on the lovely planet we call home can spearhead the gratitude cycle. This small act can fill our minds with positive reinforcement and kick-start our day, putting us in a good mood.

It only takes a quick act of self-reflection. People mistakenly seek gratitude only in extraordinary events, but not in the mundane. Certainly, extraordinary events elevate our senses and make our appreciation more vivid, but we should also appreciate every other moment. We're blessed just to be alive. We can appreciate the small moments: having a job, even if it's not our life's purpose, allows us to appreciate the opportunity to earn money, build a work ethic, and eventually move toward a more fulfilling calling.

When we lack appreciation for what we have, we only realize its value when it's gone. We may then regret not appreciating those things—our health, our shelter, things working for us every day—in the first place. It's because we are so used to these things that we take them for granted. We're incredibly lucky to even be alive—the odds are incredibly slim, but we made it through.

Our lack of appreciation for many of the things in our lives may be what holds us back and leaves us miserable. We may always be craving more, even when we have plenty to be grateful for already.

Consider your sense of sight. Most of us have had it since birth, but we never really appreciate it. What if life took our sight away forever? We'd surely want to go back and appreciate every moment we could see; even those mundane sights.

I'm not suggesting that appreciation be constantly overthought. The point is that, because life passes quickly, we should practice gratitude daily, focusing on the simple pleasures. One day, we'll be old and immobile. Appreciating the beauty of what we have and what's to come makes life more peaceful in this chaotic world.

Recalibrating the compass

Think of gratitude as the guide to what really matters. When self-reflecting, ask yourself: "What really matters to me?" Identify your personal values and goals through reflective thinking, and let gratitude for them guide your actions in life.

Like a compass, reflective gratitude makes our purpose clear and shows us the direction we need to go to achieve our goals. When we ponder how life has taken us down a path we've chosen—even if our decisions turned out badly—we can see how these decisions and actions have led to the present moment. The journey may have been rough, but reflecting on the gratitude we feel can help us determine our true purpose.

We understand the meaning behind everything through deep reflection, which, in turn, gives us the answer to start living a fulfilling life. Everyone needs to read this clearly and take it in with a focused mindset: self-actualization helps us move toward a more meaningful existence.

The societies of today's world chase money, status, and validation. We're constantly seeking more. This mindset masquerades as a path to a busy and full life, but it actually leaves us feeling empty because we're obsessing over external objects that hold no meaning.

We all need money, but when it consumes us in an unhealthy way—as it does for the majority of the world—it becomes wasteful.

Social status is the same. Why do we feel tempted to think we are better than someone because we have more than they do? We obsess over competing with other people when we should be competing with our past selves. This is why self-reflection is essential to see if these pursuits truly bring fulfillment, or if they are just empty desires we so desperately reach for to cover up our insecurities.

Many wealthy finance professionals, who lusted after money in their former years, have become so desperate in their pursuit for meaning that they've given up the industry, cashed in their money, and started living meaningfully. They've bought sailboats to cruise the oceans or have gone rural to grow organic plants and raise cattle. People who have everything often turn to simplicity in the end because that's where gratitude leads them. There's more value in it than in a chaotic world of fake lifestyles.

Living in appreciation

practicing reflection and gratitude as a daily mindset to engage with life can help build a reflective and grateful way of being. It's a perspective that brings out more of our light and less of our darkness. This helps not only our lives but also the lives of those around us. It improves mood and boosts self-esteem. Small moments of appreciation can entirely shift our mood without consuming much time.

Try it daily. You'll see your mood improve and feel a sense of love take over your soul.

Gratitude shapes how we see the world through the quality of our thoughts. Low-quality, negative thoughts keep us frustrated and lazy. If we focus consistently on gratitude, appreciation, and thankfulness, we'll have more positive thoughts and see the world with awe. In turn, we're shaping ourselves into happier people in daily life, at work, at home with our family, and in society. Others will see our auras shine because, even when others don't know us personally, our gratitude brings out our confidence.

Being actively grateful means seeing value, even during adversity. Adversity happens to all of us, no matter who we are. When we go through difficult times—a breakup, losing our house, getting fired—we should challenge ourselves to wake up, enter a state of self-reflection, and identify three things we're grateful for. Even if we're upset about being fired, we can be grateful for the opportunity we had and the skills we learned that boosted our work ethic. The unknown is scary, but if we see the beauty in it and are grateful for painful events in the past, we heal faster and move forward more quickly.

Adapting to the external world can be difficult, especially for free thinkers like us who don't follow crowds. We see the beauty in all of it, even the darkness, as we are the light that shines there. By looking within, finding appreciation, and projecting that gratitude out into the world, the universe sees, and we will receive rewards in return.

Try it and see for yourself.

Try This Now

Every morning for a month, write down 3 things you are grateful for. These things can be different each day.

Go Deeper

At the end of the month, reflect on your gratitude list and consider how keeping it has shaped you to wake up in a positive state of mind, kickstarting each day with a boost.

Remember This

Consistent daily appreciation helps us become more spiritually connected with the world. Internal appreciation deepens our perspective of the external world.

Conquer Demons

Growing up with high-performing parents, Gavin was always worried about disappointing them and not living up to their (very high) expectations. Rather than driving him to achieve, Gavin's fear of failing and of being a disappointment to his parents manifested in him only ever taking the safest option—the path he knew he would succeed at.

This fear stopped Gavin from putting himself forward for opportunities. He didn't nominate himself for house or school captain. He didn't apply for the scholarship program at university, which may have allowed him to study overseas. And he only applies for higher duties and promotions if he knows he'll get them.

Gavin's inner demon may have allowed him to avoid parental disappointment, but it has also prevented him from being as successful as he may otherwise have been.

Everyone has darkness within—that little devil on our shoulder that pushes us toward destructive paths. When we listen to it, we spiral out of control, developing mental illness, addiction, and falling into escapism. We battle these inner demons every day to stay on the path of righteousness, recovering one day at a time for the rest of our lives.

No matter what we've experienced, however, whether that be mental illness, trauma, addiction, or even criminal activity, these struggles can be overcome. Reflective thinking can guide us toward conquering our demons and winning this fight.

These inner demons are not mythical creatures. They are our deep-rooted mental, emotional, and psychological burdens. They are the destructive feelings—fear, guilt, regret, shame, hatred, and unresolved trauma—that we fall into. Common breeds of inner demons are fear of failure, insecurities, self-doubt, guilt, and addictive behaviors. Life can lead us down the rabbit hole of these feelings and eventually take us to rock bottom.

When we reach that low point, it is possible to gather our senses and pick ourselves up through reflective thinking that helps us understand how to overcome our situation. It's important to remember that this situation is temporary, and the only way to go from here is up as we fill our mindset with positive feelings. It is how we begin to heal.

None of us are perfect. We all make mistakes. Inner demons are universal, and we all have them—even your friendly neighbor down the street who looks like she wouldn't harm a fly. They should never be viewed as a weakness. Some people just manage to overcome them better than others through resilience, mental toughness, and courage developed over time.

Acknowledging our inner demons is essential to facing them. Denial won't help win this battle—it will only confuse us and lead us back into bad habits. We cannot avoid past pain if we want to grow into someone who lives a successful life.

This may be frightening, but it's a battle only we can fight. No one else can win it for us. Others can offer advice, but they have their own demons to conquer and won't completely understand ours.

If acknowledging your demons takes time, that's okay. Take all the time you need. You're healing, one day at a time.

Key Takeaway

Inner demons are not the end of life as we know it; they can be addressed through reflection and a growing understanding of our psychological shadows.

Why we avoid facing our inner demons and the cost of repression

Avoiding our inner demons causes serious damage to our mental health, creating setbacks that prevent us from living our lives to the fullest. Repressed emotions lead to self-destruction because we're not dealing with problems that are mentally eating us alive.

People build defense mechanisms—denial, distraction, and escapism—that trap them in addiction, letting them escape reality so they don't need to address their problems. When people experience something traumatic, they distract themselves with vices to forget what they've been through because it's easier than processing their emotions. This leads them down the toxic path of addiction: drinking alcohol to numb pain, using illicit drugs, gambling to chase highs, or becoming workaholics who hide their emotions behind constant busyness.

Avoiding what hurts us brings anxiety and depression.

This happened to me when I never dealt with past traumas. I remained in states of panic or melancholy. It was a horrible cycle of seeking constant highs to numb the pain I was so desperate to avoid. These inner demons originated from my external world but caused suffering in my mind.

Inner demons can manifest from various external scenarios, such as bad relationships, destructive habits, or a lack of fulfillment. These external manifestations of negative energy shouldn't be repressed. We can confront them through reflective thinking, so we don't travel down a path of destruction, but instead endure through the pain until we overcome it.

Conquering our demons isn't a simple task, but it's worth going through the healing process, because on the other side of our heartaches lies glory and freedom. We can't see this when we're going through a difficult time, and that's the trickiest part. We must believe there is always light at the end of the tunnel, even if we can't see it.

Keep enduring. Don't avoid the healing process after a horrible experience. Eventually, relief will come.

The more we avoid our inner demons, the more power they have over our lives. Consider Gavin. He didn't see it clearly, but subconsciously, he was suffering.

Bring your inner demons to consciousness so you can defeat your struggles.

The Journey Inward

Confronting our demons is a battle only we can face—and conquer. No one else can fight our battles for us; they can only provide some support and comfort. Every one of us has a warrior spirit—even the people who think they are weak, or those who are viewed as weak. Everyone has the capacity to fight; many people just can't see it.

If you are struggling with mental illness, trauma, or physical pain that brings out your inner demons and controls your mind, know that you can face them.

These struggles originate externally

The world can be unjust and unmerciful. It will do its best to tear us apart. We place pressure on ourselves to please a world that treats us cruelly. The key to overcoming that pressure is being kind to ourselves all the time.

No one will love us as much as we love ourselves

Practice self-care and demand the self-respect you deserve from others. We won't earn respect from others until we start loving and respecting ourselves. Someone who cannot battle their inner demons with self-faith cannot spread light to others until they rethink their mindset through reflection. Reflection in solitude helps us find love and respect for ourselves so we can restore our light. The light was never truly extinguished; just a little dim.

When your inner demons trigger impulsive behaviors, be compassionate

Do a good deed for a stranger without expecting anything in return. Aim for simple acts that won't drain your energy. You're not fighting someone else's battle for them; you're just giving them a helping hand.

This may sound stupid and pointless when we're at our worst, but it works. Sometimes we need to force ourselves to express compassion. We may not recognize the value of our deed when we're sad, but as we push out of our lowest point and eventually defeat our current struggles, we'll look back and see that when we were going through a hard time, we still helped someone.

When we do reach the other side and practice gratitude more significantly, we'll realize how blessed we are to have conquered our demons while performing acts of kindness during our pain. Isn't that magical?

While serving others, we can reflect on our inner demons. Defeat them by bringing life to the world.

Transformation through the fire

There's nothing better than winning a battle that determines the direction of our lives. I firmly believe two paths are written: destruction and glory—the contrast between good and evil.

Both scripts exist. But which road do we choose? The path of comfort, ignorance, and stagnation, avoiding our demons? Or the side of hope, faith, and a life worth living?

Only we can make this decision for ourselves. No one will do it for us, and no one will save us if we choose wrongly. Only we can escape.

When we confront our demons and win a battle against a particular struggle, the rewards are increased self-awareness, emotional resilience, and deeper compassion for others. We develop these virtuous traits after going through hell and surviving with many battle wounds. Negative experiences prove that pain is not the enemy—it's the teacher. Pain transforms us for the next chapter when we close the previous one, revealing life lessons. Take the pain and use it wisely to adapt to the next experience, growing stronger to handle the adventure that awaits.

These ups and downs are what make life worth living. There is no such thing as sunshine all the time. We must also suffer to learn life lessons and become stronger people.

The wisdom we gain from reflecting on all our struggles—past and present—increases every time we become aware of what the experience was like and how we defeated our inner demons. We become wiser through adversity, learning lessons we can adapt to the present and future challenges. The wisdom we gain from conquering our demons will direct us towards a path of freedom, power, and wholeness.

This is a lifelong journey. Just because we defeated those demons doesn't mean they can't return in another form through another tough experience. As long as we keep fighting, we'll come out stronger each time. As lonely as this fight seems, others can help. Loved ones who support us, professional therapy, and deep friendships make the battle worth winning.

Try This Now

Think of a small inner demon, confront it, and be truthful to yourself.

Go Deeper

Reflect on the experiences you had that involved this inner demon. Maybe they fed the demon. Maybe they were curtailed because of the demon. Focus on the feelings you associated with these experiences. Finally, look at how you conquered the demon and the associated feelings. If this negative pattern ever returns, be assured that it can be overcome again.

Remember This

We are all in this together, and we are never alone. Never give up on yourself. Keep fighting and live a life worth remembering.

Suffering

Roger started an online store, selling current trending products. It became a big success, generating a profitable weekly cash flow. Thanks to his thriving business, Roger lived a very comfortable life–until a competing company started to take over his client base, leading Roger into bankruptcy.

Roger was in shock at how quickly it had all happened. He'd had it all one minute, and had lost it all the next. Every day, the burden of his financial loss weighs him down. There is no light at the end of the tunnel and, right now, he cannot see any possible way he can pick himself up and start fresh with a new business venture all over again.

The truth reveals itself through suffering, and it's our decision how we respond to it. Will we embrace it, or will we shrink from it? Suffering reveals much about our true selves, our beliefs, inner state, attachments, ego, and self-delusions. It shows how our life experiences have shaped us negatively, leading to our suffering.

Our first step to healing is to identify the weak points that lead us to pain. When we reflect on ourselves in an effort to uncover the truth, we can pinpoint our weaknesses, begin strengthening them, and then start healing.

Pain needs to happen so we can think about how we can overcome the illusions we are blinded by. When we're suffering, everything is stripped away except our real selves, the most raw and unfiltered version of us.

We need to deal with our emotions and accept them for what they are. This is why reflection is valuable. It allows us to uncover insights into who we are and what we're looking for in life. Suddenly, the path we need to take to achieve joy and fulfillment becomes clear.

Suffering shows everything. The uncertainty is daunting. It's terrifying to think we need to self-destruct to actually find ourselves, our worth, and what is worth living, fighting, and dying for. When we go through suffering, we see what we cling to–whether it be love, validation, or identity. We are beset by our fear of loss or failure, so we repress the knowledge that loss can be inevitable, and refuse to accept it. The reality is that one day, the person we fear losing may leave our lives, and then we'll suffer and grieve.

The pain we endure is meant to be our teacher, guiding us through our low points. It may hurt, but we can choose to see how it can help us grow. In Roger's case, he'd made sacrifices to grow his business and achieved success quickly. The shock of his rapid downfall not only left him in financial pain, but he was also grieving the loss of the business he'd grown from scratch. This situation has shaken Roger's confidence, and he cannot see the point in starting over.

If we find ourselves in a similar situation, we may be able to see how all our bad traits, like fear, shame, guilt, and anger, were buried under the distraction of love. Our reflective thinking can allow us to identify all these negative traits so we can learn from this experience for our next relationship. We can be cautious about letting our fear guide our actions.

Key Takeaway

Real growth starts when everything falls apart. That's when we are truly tested. It's when we can truly see the mirror of our soul.

The nature of suffering

Suffering is a difficult trial that can make or break a person. No one enjoys it, but in this life, it is unavoidable. It's a part of human nature. Some people experience more painful struggles than others, but suffering is universal. Existential suffering can discourage us from living to our full potential when being forced to confront the core questions of our existence: the meaning of life, our purpose, and how we view death. It's spiritual distress caused by life's uncertainties. We don't know where the road will take us, and we have so little control.

Suffering doesn't live only in our minds and souls; it also takes physical form through illness and disease that inflict pain on our bodies. The root cause of our suffering is in our mind; when we are struggling with abject grief, loneliness, and heartache, the stress from these emotions physically reflects on our bodies, weakening our immune systems. It's a chain reaction of declining health that won't stop until we take action and find meaning and hope in the suffering.

Suffering isn't all there is to life, but it's an inescapable part of it. It's inevitable to face loss, experience failure, and be forced to recognize we're only mortal, and one day, we will no longer be here. Reflecting on these truths can help us accept our mortality and recognize that we are not invincible. Ultimately, we can let go of these fears so we can live our lives in abundance.

We lose. We gain. But most importantly, we have ourselves and the opportunity to live. That's enough to endure suffering, wake up to ourselves, and see the beauty in life. Most people try to avoid suffering, which is why most people don't lead meaningful lives. They remain mediocre due to their ignorance, and they do their best to live in society with their heads down, seeking no meaning from the hard truths life reveals.

Nobody has all the answers. We never will. We will only gain a better understanding through overcoming our suffering, thinking outside the box, and seeing the bigger picture of how that pain has transformed us into more aware people than those who try to avoid suffering.

The intelligent ones reflect on their suffering and see its value. It is not meaningless; there are lessons behind it. And this is the beginning of our awakening to a liberating place where we see life more clearly.

Reflecting on suffering

We can engage with our suffering consciously by approaching it with a reflective mindset where we seek to transform our pain into insight and strength. When we realize the cause of our suffering, we can use that insight to express ourselves and grow.

Self-expression during our healing can take many forms. We should try to sit with our pain and get it to work for us, rather than numbing it. We can do this by channelling our pain into our life's work. For example, if we're gifted at playing soccer, we can use the insight we gained from our suffering as motivation to become a better player.

When we undergo adversity, and it takes a toll on our bodies, we can express it through our gift. Using the example of a soccer player again, we can channel our anger and other emotions into energy on the field instead of numbing them with harmful vices like drugs or alcohol, and pushing through pain to show ourselves we're okay.

When we suffer and channel that pain fully into our craft, we achieve our best results. Obviously, we achieve even better results during positive chapters of our lives, but we have more to prove when we're suffering. We will not stop for anything, and the force is strong if we allow it to be used wisely. When we look back on these times later, we'll remember we channelled our energy into our craft rather than turning to destructive vices. This is how we get results.

Reflection gives us the courage to say, "I suffered, I learned, and I grew." We become wiser by defeating a mindset of suffering that many struggle to overcome. We make it out while others don't. We should be proud. No one can take away the strength we've built—we're beasts that defeat suffering.

It's important to remember, however, that reflecting on suffering won't erase the problem, but it does help us understand what it is and how to get through it positively. Life is difficult for all of us. We have no choice but to suffer. Even wealthy entrepreneurs living on multi-million dollar yachts suffer. They may not show it, but they bleed too. They're only human. They have their own struggles.

Know that it's okay. And just make sure you come out on the other side.

The gift of suffering

Wisdom, compassion, and purpose are the foundations for exploring the deeper meaning of suffering. This path happens for a reason, and that reason is to help us become the people we must be.

All great free thinkers, artists, leaders, and people of influence have suffered. Look at the rags-to-riches stories; many people who became successful later in life came from nothing. They had no food on their plate, endured trauma and abuse, and suffered constantly for years, yet they still came out on top. Only a small number of people make it out and go that far. And they are human, just like you. If they can do it, you too can turn your suffering into an amazing success story the world can resonate with, and give those seeking direction a source of inspiration.

It’s an amazing feeling to unknowingly be a source of inspiration. Someone could be going through a tough time, but after hearing your story and seeing how you got through your suffering, they may mirror your approach, using it as a tool to help themselves. They reflect, get to the bottom of their downfalls, and make a change–as you did. Then, they overcome it, and that was all because of you. Wouldn’t you love to be someone who helps others without knowing, possibly discovering one day that you saved a life?

This is the beauty of overcoming our own downfalls: doing so helps other people. We become effortlessly compassionate because we've already endured that struggle and shown the world. This is the gift; we beat our suffering, gain wisdom, find our purpose, and transform our lives into successful ones, helping people change their own lives with compassion.

So think: when you are suffering, will you numb your pain with vices and live in idleness? Or will you get through it, value the gift your suffering has given you, and create a spark in the world, becoming a symbol of hope for the less fortunate?

We all know the right answer, but going down the right path can be scary. Just know that if you reflect, you will grow. If you try to avoid pain, you will keep repeating these negative patterns until you decide to change for the greater good.

Try This Now

Reflect on a low point in your life when suffering had you down, clouded your mind, and made you feel pain.

Go Deeper

Ask yourself how you might channel your pain and associated emotions, turning them into motivation for change and healing.

Remember This

You can find all the meaning in the world by reflecting during times of suffering. It's not the end—it's a path; either the path of glory or the path of wrongdoing. Life is about choices. It's your choice which road you take.

Principle 6 Recap:

Write Your Own Script

Core Idea 1: Gratitude grounds your story — reflection transforms chaos into clarity.

Core Idea 2: Facing your demons is self-authorship — you reclaim control by confronting what controls you.

Core Idea 3: Suffering refines the soul — pain is not punishment, it's the forge that shapes your purpose.

One-liner reminder: *"The writer of your life isn't fate — it's you."*

Free Thinker Exercise Box

- **Morning Mirror:** Each morning, name three things you're grateful for — one joyful, one ordinary, one painful. Watch how your perspective shifts.
- **Shadow Letter:** Write a one-page letter to your inner demon (fear, shame, regret). Acknowledge it, thank it for its lesson, and release it.
- **Pain-to-Purpose Map:** Draw two columns: "What hurt me most" and "What it taught me." Connect the dots to reveal hidden growth.
- **Gratitude Pause:** When you catch yourself complaining, stop and name one hidden gift in the situation.
- **Kindness Without Return:** Do one anonymous good deed this week. Notice how giving heals your own scars.

Goal: Build the daily habit of gratitude, courage, and reflection. Turn suffering into strength and hardship into authorship.

Free Thinker Challenge (Optional)

The 7-Day Rewrite

For one week, journal each night as if you're the author of your life story. Rewrite one event — past or present — from victim to hero.

Ask: *What did this teach me? How can I use it to help others?*

By day seven, you'll realize you were never broken — you were becoming the author all along.

Principle 7: Pursue the Unconventional Path

"There were three additional rules of Einstein's work that stand out for use in our science, our problems, and our times. First, out of clutter find simplicity. Second, from discord make harmony. Third, in the middle of difficulty lies opportunity."

— John Archibald Wheeler

This final principle embodies everything that has come before it. By losing self-doubt, understanding fear through cause and effect, and confronting the logic behind ambition and drive, you gain the courage to walk a path aligned with truth—even when it defies expectation.

7 Principles of Free Thinking

Claim Your Beliefs

Curiosity Without Fear

Listen Deeper, Speak Smarter

Question Authority

Challenge Cultural Norms

Write Your Own Script

Pursue the Unconventional Path

Overcome Self Doubt

Kylie was the result of an unplanned pregnancy. Her parents were engaged to be married, and Kylie was "very much loved" according to her mother; however, Kylie was unable to reconcile these words with her mother's actions. In fact, Kylie remembers her mother once telling her, "I'm not at all maternal." Kylie grew up distant from her mother. They did not have that close mother-daughter bond that Kylie saw with her friends and their mothers. In short, although her parents were together and Kylie was provided for, she grew up feeling abandoned and unloved.

As Kylie grew older, her self-doubt about deserving to be loved intensified. She ricocheted from relationship to relationship, not for love but for security and for the comfort of having someone to depend on. Her neediness and lack of independence made her relationships unstable and only served to reinforce her cycle of abandonment.

Self-doubt ruins a person's true potential. It's what keeps us trapped in our comfort zones, too afraid to leave, lacking the drive to confidently take the risks necessary for our growth. We feel caught in a web we think we can't escape—but we can if we change our mindset. It's time to understand self-doubt and recognize it as the enemy of rational thinking.

Self-doubt is a mental habit that plagues us all; however, it is possible to learn to doubt ourselves less. Self-doubt is the second-guessing of decisions and capabilities. It sounds like: "I can't do this because I'm not good enough."

Negative self-talk must be demolished; it has to be driven out of our bodies. It destroys our rational thinking because too many negative emotions fog up our brains, making it harder to think logically. For this reason, we must not be so hard on ourselves; healthy self-questioning with humility is better than self-doubt, which leaves us feeling paralysed.

The biggest cause of self-doubt is a lack of self-awareness. We may excel in some aspects of our lives, but not in others. Asking for help with humility is key.

Doubt can stem from incidents that happened a long time ago. These incidents don't need to be as deep as Kylie's example above—in fact, they could be something much more basic—but they still spark issues people need to overcome.

Self-doubt is often the product of emotional noise. It originates both internally and externally. Internally, we might tell ourselves we cannot accomplish something because someone in the external world said so. Imagine your parents told you that you couldn't become a musician because it's too high-risk and they want you to be a lawyer like the rest of the family. Hearing this would disrupt your ability to think rationally about how you could succeed as a musician and increase your self-doubt. Negative emotions from your family can cause you to spiral into a frenzy of self-doubt because the people closest to you don't believe in you.

Key Takeaway

To beat self-doubt, don't let it get in the way of rational thinking. The only correct answer comes from reason, not from self-doubt and the negative emotions that accompany it.

The logic-based framework for challenging self-doubt

Here's a five-step framework you can use to challenge and defeat your self-doubt.

Step 1: Identify the doubtful thought

Maybe you want to learn to drive, but doubt your ability to do so. You question yourself, saying, "I can't do this," which sets you up for worry and makes you afraid to get behind the wheel. To work on overcoming this, practice self-awareness by writing down your doubts and fears, and finding the root cause so you can start driving. Awareness is always advantageous when finding solutions.

Step 2: Analyze the evidence with critical thinking

Do you have proof that supports your belief? Doubt often stems from a lack of a controlled mindset. Start questioning yourself from a more positive direction. Ask, "can there be another explanation for my fear of driving? Can I rationally think through my fears?" Perhaps there's some form of trauma. Keep questioning yourself until you form a rational explanation through analysis and evaluation.

Step 3: Evaluate the consequences

Ask yourself, "what happens if I continue with my self-doubt?" The answer will likely be: never being able to drive, which will then leave you with inconvenient ways to travel that severely disrupt your day and routine. This shows the consequences of self-doubt. Instead, have the courage to ask, "what could happen if I challenge my self-doubt?" This question can be a turning point, showing you that you can conquer self-doubt with reason.

Step 4: Reframe the narrative logically

Put an end to the false assumptions holding you back. Use reasoned statements to prove to yourself that you can drive without being afraid. Refrain from telling yourself, "I can't drive because I'm afraid and overwhelmed by traffic." Instead, say, "I've been afraid before and overcame fears from the past, and I can overcome this." Logical thinking sharpens our minds and helps us adjust our mindset without emotions getting in the way of reason.

Step 5: Take calculated action

The logic you've created in your mind must lead to action. You can't come up with a logical way to overcome self-doubt and not apply it—that's still doubt! Once you've reached a logical conclusion, follow through with actions to rid yourself of self-doubt. Confidence is built by doing, not just thinking. Apply this framework and eliminate self-doubt.

Cultivating a rational inner voice

Cultivating a rational inner voice is crucial when you're solving a problem, because we are always speaking to ourselves in our heads. We can eradicate self-doubt with reason by explaining to ourselves why we're capable of greatness rather than filling our heads with negativity and doubt. Develop a consistent inner dialog rooted in logic. Be your own logical coach, not your harshest critic. Speak to yourself as a mentor. Psych yourself up. Yell at yourself in the mirror to motivate yourself. If you need to get angry, channel it in healthy ways, like through physical activities, to release tension and achieve clarity.

Mentor yourself with explanations of who you are. Choose to be great. Don't speak to yourself as if you're your own enemy—that's your dark side trying to put you down through self-loathing and doubt, and that is no longer an option. It's time to detach from emotional spirals and speak internally in terms of facts, not feelings.

Use mental models like first principles thinking. This involves breaking down complex doubts into basic truths. For example, we may have a fear of heights that prevents us from skydiving. Rather than exhausting every detail of every experience, thought, and emotion since childhood, we can break it down to understand the problem. Focus on the worst experiences, how we felt, and how we can train our minds to overcome them.

Another mental model is probabilistic thinking. Understanding uncertainty doesn't mean we're wrong; it's about managing odds. Bungee jumping is scary, and it's possible the cord could break, but before we give in to doubt, we should look into the odds of that happening. Research the cord material. Check whether there have been any injuries or deaths at the bungee-jumping company. Review statistics on how often the cord breaks. When we do this research and gain a better understanding of the problem, we cultivate a rational inner voice. Now we'll be able to confidently say the odds are with us, and it is safer than we initially thought.

To keep our minds on track to grow our rational inner voice, we should maintain self-consistency once we have begun cultivating it. Logic will guide the kind of thinker we want to be. It's a matter of whether we want to grow or whether we'd prefer to stay in our comfort zone, remaining mediocre, like the majority of conformists in the crowd. It's important to be consistent in using our rational inner voice to be a better person every day. Not only is it beneficial for self-development, but it also reduces reactive emotions and helps us gain peace in life, which is very rare in this day and age.

Building long-term confidence through logical action

Logical action plays a critical role in building long-term confidence. We must trust our rational thoughts rather than overthinking with our hearts. We must also utilize our brains to make our actions work to benefit us.

The heart causes too much emotion, but the brain can make you more robotic. It's our choice to balance them in a healthy way to create a well-rounded lifestyle where we can think with brilliance, but also encourage ourselves to have feelings. When combined with accomplishing tasks, the balance gives us the self-control to complete them. Accomplishments gradually build our confidence in the long term. Rational thinking should not be treated as a one-time solution; it's the perseverance in building that mindset over time that gradually increases our confidence.

Confidence is earned, not granted. Some people are naturally confident, but they still have to build it up consistently for it to grow. Others need to work harder to build a confident mindset.

Being confident doesn't mean doubt is fully absent; it's the result of confronting doubt with reason and action. People will doubt us, but does that give us the right to put ourselves down with negative emotions? No! We reason with ourselves, fight back against the pain of negative energy, and take action on our journey to level up.

Your past mistakes do not define you, but they should mold you into a stronger person in the present moment. When you finally achieve a goal after failing many times, it's not fear that you vanquished; it's the fact that your decision-making has become more rational than during your previous attempts. We build confidence through resilience.

We are who we socialize with, so when we're trying to cultivate a logical mindset, we should surround ourselves with brilliant thinkers. A positive community of like-minded people helps us build a mindset that sharpens our minds for growth. This kind of socializing boosts confidence, unlike when we immerse ourselves in an environment saturated with drama, panic, and irrationality. The people we socialize with will help determine how our confidence will grow.

Try This Now

Reflect on lessons you've learned from past experiences where you succeeded. Ask yourself what actions you took when you were thinking logically. Give yourself healthy, positive feedback.

Go Deeper

Now consider your failures. Analyze them to recognize whether you were working from emotion or trying to incorporate logical actions. Reflect on past mistakes and consider how you might improve upon them in future experiences.

Remember This

The only way to overcome self-doubt is by cultivating confidence. Building resilience and intentional socialization are key, as is viewing your failures as data rather than identity.

Fear Nothing – Recognizing Cause and Effect in Fear-Based Decision Making

Derek arrives at the gym. It's his very first time. He is overweight and finally starting a journey toward health and a better quality of life. He sees many fit people in the weight section working out intensely. Their energy is high, which intimidates Derek, particularly because he has no clue when it comes to the fundamentals of lifting weights. He feels uncomfortable and is reluctant to start because he's afraid he doesn't know what he's doing.

Step by step, he edges closer to the bench press. His heart thumps, and he focuses too much on his surroundings and the other people.

Eventually, he takes a deep breath. He knows he must endure the fear in his head and begin the journey. He starts racking up the weights on the barbell.

Fear can seem difficult to overcome, but with the right logical mindset, we can conquer our fears, one at a time. Fear often originates from past experiences, when our minds identify an object or event to avoid at all costs; it signals danger and compels us to react accordingly. But ask yourself this: What am I really afraid of?

The internal cause-and-effect we create signals our bodies to panic. In Derek's case above, his initial thoughts and beliefs that he doesn't belong in the gym because he doesn't know what he's doing are the cause, while the effect is his discomfort and reluctance to begin. Eventually, however, Derek realizes that his fear is holding him back and that he has to start somewhere.

When we understand that all journeys begin with learning something new, we can let go of our fear and move on to achieving our goals. The others in the gym who seem to know what they're doing would have also had to start at the beginning at some point, and Derek is no different. This type of realization, the cause-and-effect thought pattern, is how we can work through fears and overcome them.

Most people don't understand their fears, which prevents them from conquering them. Logical thinking begins with dissecting fear and figuring out its role. Most of our fears are irrational—figments of our imagination that our minds have tricked us into believing. We create false realities that trigger negative panic reactions rather than solving problems.

Think rationally by questioning and analyzing your fears. Do they really represent reality, or are our fears distorting reality? Logical thinking is the intelligent process that shows us how to use reasoning to conquer our fears.

If we work less with emotion and more with rational thought, we can overcome our fears and move on with our lives.

Key Takeaway

Don't let past traumas dictate your present or prevent building a bright future for yourself. Let them go and begin to live.

The cost of fear-based decisions

Fear hijacks our reasoning, turning us into emotional wrecks. Emotional reasoning takes over, pushing logic out. When this happens, our minds conjure up irrational ideas that our emotions stop us from challenging. Emotional reactions create mental frenzies, leading us to jump straight to irrational conclusions and worst-case scenarios rather than thinking things through.

Fear-based decisions lead almost instantly to panic states, revealing perspectives we don't realize are unreasonable in the moment because fear clouds our judgment. We stick to our comfort zones and avoid discomfort in response to these fears. This is the wrong solution, because discomfort is necessary for growth. For example, if we fear the unknown, we might stay in a job we hate and find unfulfilling. When we don't want to face our feelings, we won't overcome our fears, and we remain in our comfort zone with no room for growth.

Fear produces regret, stagnation, and self-sabotage. Regret is difficult to swallow, especially for an elderly person who is acutely aware that their time is near its end. However, younger people with more time can start changing today. The effect doesn't always have to be negative, and that's why resilience is key. If we stay stagnant, we may get short-term relief, but that doesn't fix the problem long-term. Essentially, the only outcome is a continuous waste of our valuable time and unsatisfactory outcomes.

When it comes to cause and effect, fear-based thinking is the cause, while the life we tolerate becomes the effect. Is it worth living a life in which we make decisions based on fear? Life is precious and short, and most of our fears are untrue. Risk exists everywhere beyond our control, so we need to let go of our irrational thoughts and start living a fuller life. It's worth trying to be who we've always desired to be and to be true to ourselves.

We should never let fear drive our decisions and manifest the reality we want to avoid. We're all scared of something, but what separates the great from the fearful is that, as the former, we try our best to overcome our fears, even if it takes multiple attempts.

Don't let your safety net cost you your future. Use logical thinking to break the emotional cycle by mapping the consequences. You'll be surprised how easily you can conquer your fears.

Mastering fear through analysis

Using logic to analyze ourselves can teach us about courage. It primes our minds with positive thoughts, allowing us to reach rational conclusions and defeat the fear that has taken over our lives. If we have control over our minds, we can direct ourselves down a path less traveled, where the successful ones achieve glory.

Logical tools help us dissect our fears to uncover their true cause. Critical thinking and logic work together:

1. Ask: "What am I really afraid of?" Find the root cause of your fear.

2. Question the benefit: "What's the worst that could happen?" Thinking things through logically will likely show us that most of our fears can be overcome.

3. Use probabilistic thinking: "How likely is the worst-case scenario, really?" Look at the facts to see how high the probability of harm really is. Chances are, it's slim.

An example of this process in action might look like this: You fear public speaking. It's not like you can die from it, so when you unpack it, you realize that what you really fear is humiliation if you mess up. Maybe you were laughed at or bullied at school when you made mistakes in oral work, or maybe you're just shy. This could be the root cause, and when you know this, you can also realize that the worst that could happen is being humiliated. This may be the worst-case scenario, and while it's not nice at the time, in reality, you realize that no one will remember your speech or how well you did in a year.

Courage can give us immense clarity. Before overcoming our fears, the unknown frightens us. The courage to go through something we fear transforms the unknown into the known. Logical analysis is how we gain the courage to overcome our fear. And once the unknown becomes known, we reach clarity, realizing we were afraid and lost energy over something that wasn't as big a deal as we imagined.

Bravery bridges the gap, stripping fear of its power. The reward is clarity.

Use your imagination to build courage by breaking down worst-case scenarios step by step. For example, maybe you need to end a toxic friendship. You've had enough but are too afraid to tell them. The worst-case scenario is losing a person who wasn't right for you. Solve the problem step by step: they're toxic, it must end, tell them so, cut ties, deal with a small confrontation, and then go about your life drama-free.

It's about ripping the band-aid off so you can start the next chapter and see the bigger picture.

Becoming the cause, not the effect

Living without fear doesn't mean it's not there—it means we're tough enough to face it with the full force of our bravery. Become the cause by confronting it, feeling it, and defeating it, rather than being the effect by succumbing to a reactive state of panic. It's time to reach your full potential and become fearless.

It is possible to shift our identity from someone in a reactive state driven by fear to someone who initiates action to overcome fear. Rational thought provides us with the actions to take and produces a calm mind, giving us the confidence to act.

When we say, "I'm not the effect of fear; I'm the cause of what happens next," we are empowering our minds to start thinking rationally. This statement helps us avoid being affected by fear. We need to direct our energy into analysis to find answers guided by logic, not fear. By doing that, we'll find that everything will be okay. This is how logical thinking frees our minds. It doesn't provide a cold answer without emotion—it provides the right emotion to replace our fear through rational thought, allowing us to take back control of our minds.

It's up to us as individuals to make the right decision—will I sink or swim? If we choose to push forward, our resilience grows with each fear we conquer. When we lose fear, we rewire our identity and brain, becoming sharper, more disciplined, and growing with each round of fear we face. Resilience is an amazing trait that can take us far, and it's the key ingredient in overcoming our fears.

From a self-development perspective, miracles work when we choose the path of overcoming fear. Virtuous characteristics grow constantly when we accomplish what we're afraid of. Clarity, hope, and faith all grow as we face our fears with rationality. With this growth, success begins.

Success isn't the absence of fear—we never know when adversity will shock us to our core; we're not invincible. Success is the presence of purpose and logic. The best we can do is keep our heads up, recognize our fears, analyze the causes, trace the effects, and choose a response, not a reaction. Logical thinking is a major advantage when it comes to finding answers and building courage.

Now, get out there into the world and conquer your fears. Your battles may not always be won, but the war isn't finished. Endure all the way.

Try This Now

When you are in the moment with a fear you would like to conquer, notice when you start to feel shaky and on edge.

Go Deeper

Begin to shift your mindset when you feel these emotions trying to make you stand down. Hold onto that brave way of thinking so that fear can be conquered once and for all.

Remember This

Fearing nothing helps you think clearly. With this clarity, nothing can control you.

Lack of Ambition – The Logic Behind Motivation and Drive

Sheree has been in the same teaching job for fifteen years. In this time, she's moved up the pay scale by virtue of experience but has never applied for higher duties or promotional positions. She tells people that she's all about the teaching and the students, but in reality, Sheree is terrified of having her application declined. In her mind, there are plenty of others with equal or greater skills, so why should she bother applying if failure is inevitable?

Although she tells herself this is what she wants, Sheree sees her friends and colleagues, some with significantly less experience than she, climbing the ladder and going on to achieve great things in education. And she is starting to find herself thinking bitter thoughts.

Our beliefs shape our motivations. Negative self-talk kills motivation. In Sheree's example above, she used a false belief as an excuse for not pushing herself forward. Her self-talk about the promotion process and her anticipated outcome was negative. What she doesn't realize is that negative self-talk needs to stop if any ambition is to be achieved. She'd given up before she even tried.

Even if past failures, bad environments, and poor role models discourage us and leave us stagnant, it's not reasonable to give up on life.

Low ambition is everywhere: in casual jobs, people are working on autopilot without enthusiasm, lumbering their way through the day robotically, stagnant, and soulless. They lack the ambition to be who they truly are. Life may have let them down, but they're letting themselves down even more.

People aren't necessarily lazy—they lack a motivating mindset, which kills their drive to pursue the life they desire.

And so, they lack ambition.

We often view people with a perceived lack of ambition as putting no effort into their lives. However, lack of ambition often stems from faulty internal reasoning, not laziness. When people fail to utilize their intelligence to acquire more knowledge and think more rationally, they stagnate. Bad habits seem too hard to break, and making choices that foster a valuable mindset seems impossible—but it can be done.

Many people in prosperous countries complain about how hard life is without recognizing their privilege. People make excuses for their lack of drive when the real problem is their negative mindset. With minimal ambition, they are tricking themselves out of greatness and settling for whatever life gives them.

You are more capable than you believe.

Build up your ambition by logically dismantling the reasoning that killed it. Stop saying, "I've given up because I'm not good enough." Instead, reason with yourself positively as you say, "I can accomplish what I set my mind to," or "If it's been done before, I can do it too." Replace words that put you down with positive self-talk to attain ambition.

Key Takeaway

If your body is fully functional and you're able to earn money, you're blessed to have the opportunity to grow.

Clarity breeds drive – vague goals destroy motivation

Our minds must be clear when strategising our ambitions. What we can't define, we won't be ambitious about. Clarity leads us toward our destination. We must break down our goals logically and envision the successful outcome as clearly as we can. This will motivate us to make the decisions that drive our journey. Understanding how effort leads to results drives us to accomplish each objective.

Actionable logic plays a major role in maintaining motivation. The clearer the map, the more likely we are to move. Structuring goals logically fuels ambition with a well-thought-out plan that gives us hope, builds our faith in the plan, and inspires courageous action. We naturally fall into the ambitious endeavor.

To think ambitiously, we should give our goals substance. We can't be vague. We need to give our objectives life and excitement. There is no purpose in simply saying, "I want to be successful and make lots of money." We must process it specifically: "How will these objectives bring out the color in my life?" Contrast that simple thought with a clearer perspective: "I will start a business I'm passionate about by completing all the necessary goals so it can flourish into success, reaping rewards for my hard work." Logically breaking our goals down with passion sparks the motivation we seek. The excitement in our reasoning minimizes the lack of ambition, helping us to keep moving forward with enthusiasm.

Being vague dulls our effort and makes purpose seem meaningless. Substance counts when our life goals are on the line. Logical analysis provides the ingredients we need to stay motivated. Structuring goals logically activates our brain and broadens our horizons beyond what mediocre people do. It's important to keep fueling ambition this way and leave vague thoughts out of the equation. We can't let our fire be extinguished by blandness.

Motivation is needed, not just for a single grand gesture, but to persevere every day toward our goals. Logical thinkers show up for themselves every day to light that fire.

The feedback loop

Effort without progress kills drive, so when we acknowledge our progress, we are better able to maintain our effort. We need to stay updated on our current status, progress, and remaining tasks to complete our mission because our brains need to detect progress. Without visible progress, motivation decreases, logical thinking diminishes, and the energy to continue fades. Seeing progress, even if only minimal, provides a satisfying feeling that stimulates the brain and gives us the energy to keep going.

Ambition dies when progress isn't measured. Measuring progress is evidence we're improving, and it builds confidence that our plan is working. If we don't track our progress, our mind sees no results from our efforts, and motivation decreases. The best thing to do is to look back to prove to yourself that you are driven and putting in effort. It affirms our decision not to give up.

Ambitious people always track their progress to see how they can improve in other areas. As long as we keep putting in the effort to review what we've accomplished and make necessary adjustments to keep moving forward, we will get the best results from our work. We'll get to the point where we can easily motivate ourselves in this way.

This loop should run continuously so we stay motivated most of the time, rather than just making progress toward our goals when we feel like it. Discipline holds us together during the tedious parts of the journey, but looking back at the continuous progress we've made gives us the motivation to never give up. If we follow this simple system, we'll keep swimming and avoid sinking.

Come up with a practical way to provide feedback on your work. Tracking milestones works well. We can look back at the hard-fought battles we've won. Evaluate each step, turning it into a logical analysis of how it was achieved. We can then use this to learn about ourselves and the consistency we've maintained. This determination will drive us to win the war.

Keep that motivation rolling. Ambition grows over time until it becomes a habit. Consider achieved goals as micro-wins. Create a personal ritual when a step or goal is accomplished, such as going out to a nice dinner, or spending the day at the beach. Have a small celebration just to hype yourself up and remind yourself that you are doing a fantastic job. Give yourself credit because you've earned it. Doing all of this allows the rhythm of motivation to keep flowing. The goal is important, but it's hard to motivate yourself to pursue it when there is no joy. We are humans, not robots. We need to have some fun.

Ambition isn't endless energy; it's providing yourself with feedback to keep moving forward. Without signals of appreciation from reviewing your progress, you'll become bored and abandon success. Have the excitement to stay self-driven.

Environment and Structure

The environment we immerse ourselves in has a big impact on our ambition. Toxic environments with friends or colleagues who lack ambition and burden us with extra workload, or relationships that don't help us grow, make ambition more difficult to maintain. A resilient person with purposeful internal reasoning and a solid plan can still succeed, but poor environments can obstruct an ambitious mindset and impede success. While it's not impossible to persevere through harshness, removing ourselves from toxic environments provides better opportunities to fuel our ambition. We don't want to get stuck, and bad habits in our environment could easily lead us down that path.

Our surroundings shape what feels logical to pursue. For example, a laborer at a construction company may be doing a lot of labor-intensive work with ambitions to become a foreman in four years. He gradually builds skills through intensive labor, getting to know the trade to become competent.

However, his colleagues don't put any effort in and rely on him to complete their work. He tries to impress his boss by taking on everyone's job, showing his work ethic, drive, and ambition. The boss sees this, but doesn't acknowledge his work. He's stuck losing excess energy doing everyone else's job. As his motivation burns down to mere embers, he approaches his boss about a promotion. His boss denies the promotion application, preventing him from achieving his ambition.

What now?

The immediate first step should be to shop around at other prospering companies for opportunities at the next level. God willing, he'll get the job role based on the incredible credentials he acquired by paying his dues of hard work.

This isn't giving up.

If this situation sounds familiar, you'll know you need to use logic each step of the way to get to the next level. Sometimes the world is unjust, and others may not appreciate our value. There's no harm in seeking opportunity elsewhere if there's no room for us to grow in our current environment. When we secure a position based on our credentials and hard work, we haven't given up—we've used logic each step of the way.

Don't let your environment hold you back. Even when you've excelled in rational thinking and accomplished goals that feed your ambition, you might see growth inconsistencies due to your surroundings. It's okay to wait for better opportunities where people reciprocate your ambition. It's not selfish—it's the right thing to do, so you never become stagnant, as in your past toxic environments.

Try This Now

Sit down and write out your goals. Short-term and long-term. What is it that you really want in life? Be specific and honest.

Go Deeper

Start winning small objectives to feel your internal fire lighting up. Continue this and work on the long-term goals patiently. Build momentum so you align with your goals, flowing with life to achieve each one at its own time.

Remember This

Making changes in order to achieve your ambition is not giving up.

Principle 7 Recap: **Pursue the Unconventional Path**

Core Idea 1: Logic is your sword — clarity, not comfort, builds courage.

Core Idea 2: Fear fades when tested — every rational action cuts through illusion.

Core Idea 3: Faith and intuition refine reason — when logic meets belief, purpose awakens.

One-liner reminder: "*The unconventional path is walked with reason in the mind and faith in the heart.*"

Free Thinker Exercise Box

- **Doubt Detox:** Write down one self-doubting belief. Then, list three logical reasons it's false. Read them daily until your confidence rises.
- **Fear Map:** Identify one fear holding you back. Break it into three steps: What caused it? What's the worst outcome? What action shrinks it?
- **Ambition Audit:** Write down your top three goals. For each, ask: "Is this vague or vivid?" Then rewrite them in clear, measurable terms.
- **Real-World Test:** Take one idea stuck in your head and test it on a small scale. Replace theory with proof.
- **Intuitive Hour:** Once a week, spend 60 minutes offline in silence. Let gut instincts surface without logic. Note what feels certain.

Goal: Use logic to steady your emotions, intuition to steer you in the right direction, and courage to take the first step toward what others avoid.

Free Thinker Challenge (Optional)

The 30-Day Experimenter's Path

For one month, turn your thoughts into experiments. Each week, test out one new idea — in business, relationships, or personal growth — and document the result.

Ask: *What worked? What failed? What did I learn about myself?*

By day 30, you won't just think differently — you'll live like a scientist of your own destiny.

Part III

How to Become a Free Thinker

How you can become a free thinker

The airport terminal buzzes with a thousand people moving in the same direction—toward their gates, their schedules, and their obligations. A young woman sits alone against the wall, her laptop open but untouched. She's supposed to be boarding a flight to start the consulting job her parents celebrated, the one that checked every box on someone else's list. Instead, she's frozen, feeling the weight of a life that doesn't fit. In her chest, something whispers: This isn't yours.

That whisper is where everything begins.

In a world full of conformity, society drifts from the truth. We're told a version of life that makes us comfortable and dull, then congratulated for fitting it. It's time to fight for our beliefs, our purpose, and our journey—time to become an independent free thinker. Let's get uncomfortable.

Imagine living your life in a way that earns the respect of higher powers.

It all starts with finding our beliefs—and then sticking with them, refusing to let anyone disrespect our views. This is our life, and our way of seeing. realizing this and committing to it is a major turning point in our journey toward seeking and finding our purpose.

Somewhere in all of us, there's a master plan, and it's created for us to accomplish. We may not see it clearly right now, but we can feel it. Intuition tugs at us, even while outside opinions try to cloud our thinking and drag us back into their noise.

The answer comes from within; that is why I am a major believer in solitude.

We don't need to put huge amounts of pressure on ourselves. If we are taking a while to find our purpose—our answer—it will reveal itself eventually if we keep seeking, especially when we know it's time for a life revolution.

Be patient.

When the answer does come, that's when our journey begins. And it will be both messy and beautiful. It will be mixed with success and setbacks, hope and doubt, laughter and tears. We should prepare our hearts for the positive, as well as the negative. We'll need them both.

Curiosity

Curiosity becomes our first companion.

The critical thinker asks "How?" and "Why?"—not to look smart, but to see clearly. Questions let us enter the logic of a problem and the mind of the person explaining it.

Curiosity helps us gain a deeper understanding of what is being explained. A topic may be of importance to us in terms of what we are learning or trying to become.

That is why mentors are great. We can draw on their opinions and insight to come to our own conclusions about what we have learned.

The type of knowledge we seek is all about tapping into the unknown aspects of our views on a topic to expand our intelligence.

If we use curiosity in a practical way, it can work to our advantage. Never be shy about asking questions, even if they seem irrelevant. To expand our minds, we must practice curiosity so we can learn.

An apprentice car mechanic doing his first service on a car may be curious about the steps needed to carry out the task. He asks the tradesperson. The tradesperson shows, tells, and teaches the apprentice how to do the job. Being curious and asking questions brings the apprentice a step closer to being a competent mechanic and also helps his boss turn a profit.

As long as we are curious about how a task is done, we are doing great work. It may take us a few attempts to get the skill right, but this is alright because everyone is on a different wavelength in their thought processes.

Curiosity can take us a long way on our journeys as free thinkers. The more we ask, the more we will know and grow.

We should always listen more than we speak.

So many people struggle with the skill of listening rather than speaking, but it's a significant key allowing us to open the doors to answers. As a communication technique, listening is so underrated; yet it is so effective.

When we're out, it's best to keep our vanity to a minimum and listen to what others have to say. Let people talk. Imagine the knowledge we could gain just by listening. After listening and observing, if we go back to reflect, we can then gain our own understanding of the situation.

The main point of all this is listening, understanding, and learning. We may be tempted to ask a lot of questions or contribute to the conversation if the speaker has a professional background in our topic of interest, but even then, it's best not to go overboard with talking. Instead, just observe.

When we actively observe, our minds store information more accurately. We become free thinkers by gathering the information we have learned by listening to others, take all this knowledge and information, and use it in a practical way, with our own interpretation.

When we have the knowledge, we can think independently about how to use it and then apply it to our experiences. If we keep repeating these patterns and find our own way to do things that work for us, we can grow to our full potential. We gain an abundance of knowledge over time in this way, becoming an intelligent free thinker.

Questioning authority

Questioning the authority figures in our lives is about learning to step up to anyone in an authority position and stand up for what we believe is right. The ability to do this is especially important when the situation we are facing is unjust. In all cases, we need to stand our ground, not necessarily to cause trouble, but to present our case.

It’s okay to be a rebel; we just need to make sure we back up our claims with proof and take action righteously. If we know something is wrong, do we have the courage to stand up for what is right, even if it’ll cause a little friction?

It’s okay to be true to ourselves. But it's not good to overdo it and risk losing our jobs by correcting our boss. Instead, it's a good idea to be more insightful and select our battles.

Constant battles can be mentally draining. They aren't worth it. When questioning authority as a free thinker, we are going against the grain, and many people despise that.

Don't worry if you face some backlash for standing up for what you believe. The mediocre succumb to authoritarian figures because it is the path of least resistance. Never feel discouraged when you are in a battle on your own, as a free thinker.

When you have an opinion that you really believe is true, it's honorable to stand up for yourself. However, if someone proves you wrong, be humble and accept the correction. Ultimately, be cautious when going into battle, and ensure your knowledge is backed up with evidence.

Question cultural norms

How do you view the society you are part of?

We all question the rules of how our society works and the ideas and actions of those who run it. However, when it comes to truly evaluating society, most people are very basic in their critique, tending to be largely ignorant of the important social matters—crime, poverty, tyrants, and so on—that affects us in negative ways.

Even when people notice certain issues, they tend to sweep them under the rug, refraining from questioning cultural norms, or just following the trend and repeating what the majority says.

The free thinker questions the issues they notice.

One such social issue is how social media is affecting children, distracting them and making them more introverted. That's a cultural norm many of us have accepted, and it hurts us. The free thinker has every right to question this matter and spread awareness with their thoughts to educate others.

Spreading awareness by challenging cultural norms makes our society a safer, more productive, and healthier environment, allowing us all to have better quality of life as a community.

Do you see how free thinkers can become the hero?

This is how a positive revolution can happen.

If you really believe you can be a leader—if you believe you can help—then your courage to speak your own thoughts can not only be personally beneficial;

it can assist others and create a positive spark in our society, and even the world.

Continue questioning cultural norms. Go into the world to create a positive outlook about right and wrong. Don't live a script written for you by others.

Although we all have early influencers—parents, guardians, teachers—everyone's upbringing is unique. Some people with very negative influences turn out to be wonderful humans; some people with positive influences turn out to be destructive individuals.

The hardest script to reject is the one written by people who love you. Parents, teachers, and mentors might want good things for you, but often it's through their lens, not yours. They might push you toward a career in medicine when you're meant for music, or toward stability when you're built for risk. Their intentions are kind, but their vision is limited. There are certain things only you can feel: the pull of your purpose, the shape of your potential. If you live their dream while ignoring your own, you will breed a quiet, corrosive resentment. Your life is too short and too precious to waste performing someone else's hopes.

Real happiness requires that we all become our true selves—how we work, how we love, how we show up. We can use our free-thinking spirit to examine the roles we've been assigned, then keep what aligns and let go of what doesn't.

Wake up to your own life and live it.

Pursue unconventional paths

Pursuing unconventional paths is not for the faint-hearted. The weak do not stand a chance; they'll drown in adversity. Only we can decide if we sink or swim. These paths are terrifying, but very rewarding. The mediocre path of birth, school, dead-end job, marriage, kids, retirement, is sincerely overrated. An unconventional path makes it all interesting.

As a matter of fact, we can add in all the mediocre paths, and then enhance them in unconventional ways.

Look at the humans who took an unconventional path, such as Steve Jobs, the founder of Apple. This is one of the biggest companies ever, and it revolutionized the tech industry and the world. What an inspiring story he has.

Then there's the path of an average human who works a nine-to-five job—either white-collar or blue-collar. This is nowhere near as satisfying as Steve Jobs' path.

And this path is no joking matter.

Along this path, the journey is hard. There will be a lot of sacrifice, pain, and suffering—but it is deeply rewarding. By pursuing an unconventional path, you will succeed in following your purpose.

Lead by crafting your own point of view, then prove it with legitimate evidence. This is how a free thinker channels their knowledge, wisdom, and virtues into their field of work to succeed. You will make a lot of mistakes; it's not for the weak. In the long run, you will be rewarded based on the quality of your work.

Become a person of value

Once we've figured out who we are and what we stand for, we have something to offer: perspective. Help others find their own path. We can share what we've learned, not as dogma but as possibility. It's important that we're generous with our hard-won wisdom.

This is how you become a person of value. Build yourself up, then reach back out to uplift others. Share your failures as readily as your successes, because the failures contain the lessons. Show people that thinking for yourself, while difficult, leads to a richer life—better decisions, stronger identity, genuine inner freedom. Plus, if you've experienced what they have been talking about, then you'll be more likely to be able to help them.

Free thinkers help when asked, but know that, sometimes, it's okay to be reserved and save energy for yourself. As much as you would love to help and show kindness, make sure you show the same love to yourself first.

It's not easy. You will struggle mentally and find it difficult to help others and become a person of value. Looking after yourself first before lending a helping hand is essential.

How does free thinking lead to better decisions?

To know what is a better decision, we need to consider our experiences of making right and wrong decisions. The experiences we continually go through shape our decisions, actions, and boost our characteristics, especially when we make decisions that unintentionally lead to failure. We learn, and we move on. This sparks growth in strength within ourselves.

The more we fail and rise back up, the stronger we become, which leads us to overcoming adversity and becoming more competent decision-makers through these experiences. The more we project our thoughts to the world, especially if we have the confidence to be a competent decision-maker, the stronger our identity will become.

Do you understand the significance of having a stronger identity?

From the powerful personal status you have built up for yourself, people will be honest in giving you respect. The people will love you. With people on your side, you can absolutely gain a stronger identity and sense of power. This is how people take control of whatever they're involved in—business, politics, or even the criminal underworld.

Once you identify yourself as a strong human being, people will notice your magnetism—that intense aura that captivates them. You will be able to convince people to take your side in whatever you're involved in, and you can step up to the most eminent person and even take over the industry. You never know. Once you succeed in knowing and being comfortable with your true self, you will attain inner freedom.

Better decisions come from experience, including painful mistakes. Each failure teaches us something conformity never could. Over time, we develop judgment that others lack because they've never tested their own thinking. Our identity strengthens because it's built on truth, not performance. People sense this. They respect authenticity even when they don't understand it. And inner freedom? That's the prize. It's the ability to wake up and know that our life belongs to us, that our choices reflect our values, that we're not trapped in someone else's story.

Of course, most people won't understand us at first. People will often misunderstand and label us as weird. This may be a difficult situation to overcome if we're not used to being misunderstood. But once we get past that adversity, we'll know why and be glad we accepted that the general masses didn't understand us and thought we were weird.

People are so caught up in following social norms that they won't appreciate our uniqueness until we are rich, successful, powerful, and well-respected. This is difficult to deal with in the beginning, but once we pull through with a very successful life, people will realize they were wrong about us. Only then will they apologize for their error in judgment.

The best revenge is enormous success. No one will believe us in the beginning. They won't understand our master plans, often telling us we're crazy. But then we'll feel the immense satisfaction of proving all of them wrong.

It's important to always persevere in following our path and being true to ourselves, no matter how weird people may think we are, because they can't understand our vision. But it's important to focus on staying determined so we don't lose our true identity. This sounds simple, but it can be hard when so many convincing-sounding opinions are thrown around.

Fight for your principles. Don't let the naysayers discourage you.

Naysayers throw around words like impractical, weird, and naive. Let them. Their confusion says more about their limitations than ours. The masses are conditioned to follow, to fit in, to avoid standing out. When we refuse to play that game, we become incomprehensible to them—until we succeed. Then, suddenly, we're a visionary. Then they claim they always believed.

Don't wait for their approval. Don't soften your vision to make others comfortable. Stay determined. Protect your principles. And when everyone tells you you're crazy for chasing something they can't see, remember: they can't see it because they stopped looking inward years ago. You're still searching, still building, still becoming. That's not crazy. That's courage.

So if everyone thinks you're weird, and your life is elevating, the answer is simple: Stay weird. One day, they'll understand.

The woman in the airport closes her laptop. She picks up her phone and dials. When her parents answer, her voice is steady: "I'm not getting on that plane. I need to tell you what I'm going to do instead; what I actually want to do." Her hands shake, but her heart knows this is right. She's choosing discomfort over dishonesty, uncertainty over a life that isn't hers. She's thinking for herself.

This is where journeys start—with one choice to listen to the voice inside that says *this is mine to figure out.* Trust it. Question everything. Stay curious. Listen more than you speak. Stand up for what you believe. Reject the scripts that don't fit. Pursue the path that calls you, even if it terrifies you. Help others once you've found your way. And build a life so true to yourself that even when they call you weird, you'll smile, knowing you're finally free.

Remember This

The greatest betrayal isn't disappointing others—it's abandoning yourself to please them.

Your Challenge

Identify one area where you're living someone else's script. Write down what you actually believe about it. Then take one small action this week that aligns with your truth, not their expectations.

Test Hypotheses in Real-World Scenarios

From theory to action—the gap between thinking and doing

Hypothetical thinking activates the logical side of your mind, but it's not enough to fuel ambition unless you take action. Showcase to the world how your concepts work in practice, not just in theory. If you don't put your reasoning into action, it remains merely a thought, which is meaningless to everyone.

There's no room for comfort on the road to fulfilling your purpose, especially in the beginning. People develop brilliant theories with sound logic, creating opportunities for breakthroughs and executable plans. Yet they often stop short of actually implementing them. Remaining still only feeds self-doubt and accomplishes nothing. Don't let logical thinking remain stuck in your mind—activate it through experience. Testing your hypothesis in real-world scenarios helps you find solutions that you would never discover through ideation alone. Test your assumptions to minimize the risk of your dream becoming nothing more than a dream.

Testing is the next logical step to implementation, providing evidence that proves your logic is correct. Consider a science experiment: you develop a hypothesis, then take action by forming it into an experiment. If your experiment succeeds, that theory has now been proven as fact. That's when you publish a scientific paper.

The journey toward greatness follows a similar pattern:

1. Form a hypothesis.
2. Take action to prove your logic is correct.
3. Create the physical work that becomes fact.

The world will now see your success.

This all ties into the Principle 7 chapter about self-doubt. Start trusting your logical mind, take the action you need to prove your theory works. Leaving your ideas as theory won't get you very far. Harness your ambition and put in the effort to make your rational thinking come to life. Are you curious enough to test your logic? The decision is yours, but do not paralyse your mind with overthinking, as it only leads to an overload of logical data that will send you into a frenzy.

Relax.

Trust in your work.

Have the confidence to test your hypothesis in the real world.

The scientific method for everyday life–how to form and test hypotheses

Being practical with a hypothesis is how you grow belief and plan assumptions that yield results. Follow a step-by-step process to resolve theory into action:

1. Observe a problem of keen interest.
2. Formulate a hypothesis that predicts what will happen.
3. Test this hypothesis through experimentation.
4. Analyze the outcome of the experiment, leaving room for adjustments if there are any you need to take.

Let's look at a simple example where you might be thinking that waking up at 5 am will make you more productive.

1. Observe the problem of sleeping in and not having a full morning.
2. Hypothesise that waking up at 5 am will increase your productivity and abundance.

3. Test your hypothesis by waking up at 5 am for two weeks.

4. After two weeks, analyze the outcome. It works, but needs a slight adjustment: wake up at 6 am for an extra hour of sleep, creating the perfect routine.

Breaking down problems step-by-step in this way leads to proper solutions. Experimenting with a hypothesis allows us to put our ideas into practice to get the right answers. Why leave a promising logical thought to collect imaginary dust in your mind when you can experiment with it practically? You never know what could come out of it.

Jumping straight into the deep end isn't always helpful, however. Take it slow with bigger tests. Start with micro-testing to get into the routine of turning nothing into something. Gather information. Repeat this process continuously for more results. Doing this should keep your momentum flowing, maintaining your motivation and enthusiasm. Once you get the engine started, you will want to push for more results.

When testing hypotheses, don't act blindly; be cautious and validate a reasoned plan. Make sense of what you're doing. You can't come up with something unreasonable and expect it to work based on magical thinking. Work within reasonable bounds. You won't win a million dollars at a casino in one night just because you read a book on gambling. Keep in mind you're taking calculated risks, not gambles.

Feedback is data–listening to reality without ego

Ego interferes with logical thinking and achieving your mission.

Be honest with yourself

You must drop stubborn, one-dimensional opinions and be honest with yourself when something isn't working as expected. When logical thinkers test ideas, they observe the results dispassionately. Too much emotion can lead us to react stubbornly, especially when we're too passionate. When tests fail, and we can't see why, ego gets in the way, and we become stuck in biased viewpoints. Being dispassionate means letting go of ego to rectify issues. When you're right, you don't work from a place of high emotion—you simply get the job done so momentum continues and your mind stays focused.

You can't always be right

The key to dropping ego when testing hypotheses is letting go of any emotional attachment you have to being right. This is crucial, as it can derail your progress. Remember that you'll never be right all the time. If you have that mindset, it's not confidence—it's ego. Don't think you're better than you are. Maintain a humble attitude so you can accept you'll make mistakes along the way. Stay focused and endure the ups and downs of being both right and wrong as you make progress.

Work with humility

Life doesn't care about your logic—accept that to defeat your ego. We must adjust our thinking based on proper evidence because that's what the world wants to see and learn from. If you're too stubborn to accept you're wrong, you will keep repeating logically inconsistent actions that don't help anyone. Have the humility to know when you need to make adjustments to your reasoning. Even the greatest logical thinkers are humble enough to admit when they're wrong and rectify it.

Isaac Newton's laws are the foundation of physics. But then Einstein came along and developed his theory of relativity, showing that time and space weren't fixed as Newton believed, but flexible. Newton's reasoning was brilliant, given the resources and observations he was working with, but Einstein didn't cling to assumed certainty. He tested and updated the hypothesis. I'd like to think that if Isaac Newton had been alive to see Einstein's work, he would have been humble enough to accept it, but we'll never know.

Track your logic: ideas, hypotheses, results, and learning. You won't be perfect, but maintain consistency with this feedback so you're not driven by ego.

Practice what you preach–the power of living your logic

Self-belief means understanding your logic as certainty. When you've proven something as a fact and made it a major part of your life, you have a stronger message to share with others. If you truly believe your work is credible after testing your hypothesis, you have every reason to say as much. Walk the talk so others see your confidence in your work. Let them analysze and evaluate your evidence so they can know it is the truth. Logical thinkers don't just believe their proven hypotheses are clever—they embody them so others see they're on point.

Confidence grows through consistency. No matter what goal you are pursuing, when your world becomes a field of tested truths, your confidence continues to strengthen, and your ambition maintains consistent momentum. This isn't because you think you're always right—confidence grows when you repeatedly fail and succeed. It's how we learn.

Intelligence, grit, and resilience grow through time. The ups and downs give you confidence when there's no option but to keep going. Adopt a healthy obsession driven by the ambition to succeed, and this way, you'll always have a surplus of ambition.

The perks of this intense drive include the long-term benefits from hard work. The logic you put into action produces real-world results, whether you're changing your industry's standard of growth, building a healthy family life, or becoming more intelligent in general. Better decision-making plays a major role in mindset growth.

My personal favorite long-term benefit of pursuing success is having absolutely no regrets about trying. Through success and failure, nothing should knock you down if you're willing to live abundantly to fulfill your purpose. If you give up on your dream, you'll look back in regret, sad that you gave up and never saw what could have resulted. You'll question yourself, thinking about what could have been.

Never give up. Fuel your ambition to keep going. Even if it doesn't work, rather than giving up early in the process, you can move on to another venture that leads toward success.

Never lack ambition.

You never know where your life could end up.

If you remain consistent in a rational way, you'll get far.

Follow a Step-by-Step Approach

Logical thinking

Time to discuss my favorite style of thinking: logic. I have always had a keen interest in personal analysis, which has enabled me to present my reasoning to the world. I find joy in explaining my rational points of view to others in a way they can resonate with. This is how I form connections in conversations; people find my logic intriguing.

But enough about me. Let's talk about following a step-by-step approach to thinking logically.

Establishing well-structured thought sequences helps us make sound decisions and solve problems. Logical thinking needs structure to work. We think creatively by developing concepts. When we think logically, our minds gather all the ideas and chaotic thoughts that have no particular form and mashes them together, bringing them into order. Once we combine this with critical thinking, through questioning and evaluation, we reach conclusions that solve problems via reasoning.

Our brains prefer order and patterns. The structures we build in our minds make it easier to develop solutions that we can explain to others in detail. A step-by-step approach aligns with our mental framework.

These systems of patterns we follow are useful in conveying our reasoning to others. A step-by-step thinking structure might look like this:

1. Define a major goal, such as starting a business.

2. Break it down: plan market research, set short-term goals, learn the service, and launch the company.

3. Create tasks: build a client base and establish a timeline to reach long-term goals.

4. Take action.

By systematically completing the steps, we rationally connect all the dots to reach the ultimate goal. There are problems to solve at each step, and that is when great logical thinkers begin their process to achieve different objectives along the way.

The value in the step-by-step thinking process lies in the clarity it helps you achieve. We need to break down complex problems that linger in our minds. It's amazing that our brains can store all that complexity, but we need to break it into small, manageable chunks to prevent overwhelm and mental fatigue.

Step-by-step thinking allows us to organize everything in a neat structure, meaning we can solve problems more easily and continue moving in the right direction, rather than taking random chunks out of the problem.

Why step-by-step thinking works

Let's examine the anatomy of a step-by-step process using the example of writing a book like this one.

Step 1: Identify the goal

The goal is simple: write a self-help book. The purpose is to inspire readers through the principles they learn from the book. The vision for the book is that the information will be valuable in positively changing someone's life, creating a life-changing opportunity for the reader. Lastly, it should be a quality read that entertains the reader.

Step 2: Gather and verify information while avoiding assumptions

Research how readers can adapt the principles and apply them in their lives, thereby gaining the insights needed to be inspired and grow their mindset. Research is essential so the author knows what they're talking about. There should be no wild assumptions. Everything should be fact-checked. The work will still be original, but it should also be helpful and factual.

Step 3: Break the problem into smaller parts

Organize the chapters in the book, creatively shaping them into a system of knowledge. With the basic concept for the book already determined, the chapters will provide structure for systematically writing the words. This step includes coming up with chapter titles and arranging them in the right order. It's the most interesting part.

Step 4: Prioritize the sequence

Place the chapters in a logical order that makes sense and flows pleasantly for the reader. Fill in an outline for each of the chapters so you can come back to writing them later, then develop key points once you've figured out the content. It's important to plan what you're going to write before you write it. Keep the structure simple, but interesting. It's a delicate balance.

Step 5: Determine decision points and checkpoints

Decide when to evaluate or adjust the book. Set a fair deadline for completion. As you go, decide whether changes are needed, though, preferably, write the entire book first, and then evaluate by going through second and third drafts to polish grammar and content. Complete the evaluation to give life to the book in its truest form, then take that beautiful work of literature and publish it.

This is a basic anatomy of the logical step-by-step process for any author writing a book. A logical thinker needs to proceed by following a system like this in any field of work.

Obstacles to following a process and how to overcome them

To be an extraordinary logical thinker, we must try to explain our analysis while communicating our most accurate answer. There's an enormous factor at play here as we must face obstacles that block clear thinking and reasoning. People often abandon logical processes due to obstacles, so the key is to maintain discipline.

Three common mental blocks interfere with logical thinking:

Impatience

You naturally want to get your point across quickly, but if you hurry, you may skip steps in your full explanation. It's important to take your time and stay focused to stay on track. Impatience makes you seem unintelligent. Instead, stay relaxed and focus on getting your point across.

Distraction

This creates a mental block, which can make you forget what you're talking about and effectively abandon your logic. Once you remember, you have to go through the entire process again from the first step. This is exhausting, especially when explaining something complex with substantial content in your analysis.

Ego and overconfidence

People struggle with ego and confidence, but refuse to accept this out of pride. Egotism causes you to skip steps when following a process. Cockiness leads to making statements like "I know this" when reasoning with someone. Perhaps someone is showing you a different squat technique in the gym and explaining how to do it. Being cocky, you assume you already know how to do it and totally disregard the other person's advice. When you attempt the squat, your shoddy approximation of the technique results in injury. Your ego impeded you from learning a new, safer technique. Drop your ego. Stop thinking you automatically know everything and are great at everything. Be humble enough to learn from someone with experience.

When approaching situations in a step-by-step manner, be mindful of the obstacles you may face. This applies to many scenarios, but especially when you're starting up a business. Missing steps will lead to poor execution, which could put you back to square one. It's just not worth cutting corners.

Practicing step-by-step thinking in everyday life

Step-by-step thinking makes your life easier by creating a system that helps you breeze through problems. It works practically and encourages you to form better habits. Following a step-by-step guide gives you a proper routine. Making micro decisions can brighten your day and give you a dopamine hit.

As an example, let's apply step-by-step thinking to cooking. You might start by deciding to eat better because you want a healthy lifestyle. The next step is to buy the food. The step after that is to cook it the same day so it's fresh. And just like that, you've achieved your end goal of enjoying a healthy home-cooked meal.

Instead of being lazy and wasting money on low-quality fast food, you could form this simple habit and be well on your way to achieving a balanced lifestyle.

The opposite of micro-decisions is macro-decisions. What are the long-term goals you strive for? For example, you might have an exercise goal to run ten kilometers in 45 minutes. To achieve this goal, you create a 3-month exercise plan. You start with 15 minutes of running for the first few days and gradually increase to 30 minutes by the end of the first week. By the end of the second week, following this plan, you'll be running for an hour.

By logically explaining how you'll reach your goal, you give yourself the motivation to put the plan into action. In three months, you will have achieved your goal. By thinking logically, you're learning and training daily to advance.

These steps are based on a compounding effect. You build yourself up each step of the way and prime yourself to gain confidence, determination, and grit. These traits are key to developing a strong mindset. We experience the effects of a healthy dopamine hit when we accomplish a single step. This gives us the confidence to keep going and drives us to get more hits, turning the goal into a healthy obsession. It means we strive for more, enduring pain along the way to get our reward. You can't tell me that isn't a huge confidence booster.

Even if it seems to be robotic, logical thinking is anything but. The process empowers us to be more intelligent, freeing our mental space for creativity and intuition once we handle the steps. Try it with something in your daily life—even a small goal like cooking. Set a short-term goal and apply a step-by-step process to complete it. Challenge yourself and accomplish the goal.

Trusting Intuition: From Gut Feelings to Spiritual Knowing

Understanding the nature of gut feelings

The brain is a wonderful organ that enables us to explore a world of wonders through our conscious and subconscious minds. The brain processes vast amounts of information beneath conscious awareness, creating what we call gut feelings. We don't see everything rationally in an instant. Information in our subconscious is where gut feelings begin. This subconscious processing draws on stored experiences and patterns to give us answers without requiring rational analysis.

You've likely experienced this when choosing a driving route. Your intuition, accumulated over many days of driving down these roads, tells you which route is fastest without needing to consciously calculate it. There's no need for a rational explanation; your gut knows the quickest direction, so you take that route. When you get there, you are proven correct.

This is just a simple everyday example. Intuition is always at work as the brain is constantly active while we are conscious. Our stored experiences guide us to the quickest answer without relying directly on logic. It's incredible how our brains work!

Relying on our intuition also protects us from danger. Our gut feelings quickly signal when something isn't right or doesn't add up. We don't need to delve deep into our minds to evaluate a situation.

Imagine you are running a construction contracting business and are meeting with a builder to close a deal for their next four projects, providing three years of work for your company. During the meeting, the builder tells you about a wonderful opportunity you'd love to be part of, but something seems off. His body language is odd. He has a deceitful look in his eyes. And he's overexcited about "turning you into a millionaire overnight."

Your intuition is sending you strong signals that this man is not as honest as he pretends. Your body weighs in, and you start to feel physical tightness and discomfort. There is no logical reason why you shouldn't trust him, but something about his energy is off. When the meeting is over, you choose to trust your instincts and decide not to take him up on his offer. Much later, you find out from a mutual friend that he was a con artist, and had you taken the deal, it would have blown up in your face.

Your intuition just saved you from a dangerous situation. This man only wanted to use your expertise and energy to his advantage.

Intuition is the cousin of bias; it works for you rather than against you. It's important to think things through logically, but sometimes you just need to trust yourself when your body signals that something is wrong.

The cost of ignoring your Gut–lessons from not listening

What happens when we ignore our intuition?

When an opportunity arises, and your gut immediately knows that this could be life-changing … but you decide to pass on it, the cost is regret. While we'll never know ahead of time whether opportunities will work out, our intuition gives us a strong signal one way or the other.

Imagine you're a 21-year-old mechanic seeking the adventure of a lifetime. You've been stuck in the same city since birth, and you've had enough. You want to explore the world. You continue working your job, but the days are repetitive and tedious. Then, out of nowhere, a friend approaches you about an opportunity to travel with him and three other friends on a two-month trip to Europe. It's the trip of a lifetime! It's exactly what you were seeking: a long trip in Europe with four of your best friends. You may never get all your friends together again for a trip like this.

Your gut feeling is amazing—you're getting all the positive signals, and the answer is right there with no reason to think about it. However, you do think about it. You contemplate how you have one year left of trade school, and you don't want to miss classes that could put you a year behind in getting your license. As hard as it is, you decline.

Months later, you see your friends posting photos of their amazing trip on social media. They're having the time of their lives. You feel instant regret for not going, knowing with certainty you should have taken the opportunity and done an extra year of catch-up in trade school.

Let's go deeper into the future. You are now 30 and working as a mechanic. You have only been on short holidays with just one of your friends, and although you are grateful for it, you now realize that an extra year of trade school could have been put off. It wasn't that important, but that trip would have changed your perspective on life, and you chose not to follow your gut. You ignored your intuition. Logically, you thought it made sense to finish trade school rather than go on the adventure of a lifetime. Not following your gut cost you that opportunity.

Be aware of the costs of ignoring the gut. Our bodies know what we desire. When we feel lots of positive energy in the face of a new opportunity, we should listen. It's so important to enjoy the journey of decision-making when it comes to following our intuition and embracing the excitement it brings as the answers become clear. Just make sure there are no regrets when an opportunity is allowed to slip by.

How to hear it–creating space for intuitive signals to arise

Intuition rarely arrives when we're sitting and waiting for it. We can try our best to force intuitive thinking, but that just leads to frustration and mental fog. We'll tire of waiting for it to come. But the moment we stop anticipating it, intuition can suddenly arrive. It's interesting how it works. Instead of forcing it, we need to create conditions for our intuitive insights to surface naturally.

Leave frustration behind

Form a sense of stillness in your mind, body, and soul to help you remain calm. This creates space for your intuition to start working on finding answers for you, giving you that "aha" moment.

Never rush for answers

Rushing decisions and solutions only creates mental fog, leaving you lost. Sometimes, it's hard to reason things out, but stillness allows us to think more clearly and search within ourselves for answers. Stillness is valuable when things become too chaotic, and you need to slow down your life. It's common to get caught up in the rat race to achieve success, but it can take a toll on our ability to express our thoughts freely. Trying to get everything done all at once and find all the answers is too much.

Make time to reset

At a time when the hustle and bustle of life feels overwhelming, it's crucial to spend time on hobbies and activities that you enjoy instead of taking everything so seriously. Life isn't meant to be so intense. Calm down. Take time for yourself so you can hear your intuition calling out to you, guiding you through the steps you need to take to keep moving forward and live a healthy life.

Engage in mindless tasks

A great way to put yourself in a state of mind to hear your intuition is to engage in mindless tasks, like cleaning your house. While you mop the floor, vacuum, and wipe down your kitchen top, you get your body moving without putting any pressure on your mind to think deeply. This helps your thoughts flow more easily. As you listen to music while you clean, actually enjoying the moment, an insight from your subconscious will suddenly surface. You finally have a clear answer to something that has been on your mind for weeks, such as why a work colleague was suddenly rude to you. As you clean, your subconscious connects the dots and brings the answer to light. If you were doing a task that required a lot of thinking, that sudden clarity may not have arisen.

The nature of spiritual intuition

Spiritual intuition comes from the divine. It's a deeper sense of reality that gives you insights without conscious thoughts; you just receive the answer, and it all makes sense. It may seem strange at first. You may not understand what's happening, or you may be afraid because these spiritual intuitions can be overwhelming and seem unreal. However, they must be embraced, as these experiences are especially likely to come your way when you are going through a hard time. You can find the answers if you pay attention to the signs, and especially if those signs come from a feeling.

However, we must be careful not to confuse emotional impulse with intuitive wisdom. Sometimes, we overthink and believe we are spiritually connecting with the divine, rushing toward an answer. Unfortunately, it isn't that easy. If we are being impulsive and try our 'luck', we won't get an answer instantly. Patience is a virtue when we're trying to make our spiritual intuition work for us. We can't force it; it simply comes when we are in a positive frame of mind. That means being in a state of stillness, the calm after the storm. That's when we get our best answers from the divine–after we have cooled down from an intense experience. Spending time in solitude, in quiet silence, helps clear our minds so we can openly channel our intuition without distractions.

The ability to tap into the deeper knowing is very important, especially if you don't understand your intuition. A spiritual person with experience channelling their intuition can do it more often. Even when they are physically present at a meeting, they can somehow tap into their minds and gain that deeper insight. It sounds hard to believe, but I know it's possible from firsthand experience and through hearing stories of other people's experiences.

Note how spiritual intuition contrasts with both logic and emotion, showing different ways the human mind perceives truth. They all offer a unique method of interacting with information, but have very different functions. Spiritual intuition derives not from thinking or emotional feelings, but from a quiet inner clarity. It's the feeling in our gut that gives us insight without conscious thought and affords us instant clarity.

In some cases, it takes a while to arrive at an answer when working through a problem in a logical order. Spiritual intuition allows a deeper connection to something greater than yourself and gives you the answer you need much faster. The beauty behind the mystery of spirituality is that we don't know how it truly works. My advice? Be grateful when you receive the blessings you seek, and follow through with the solution. Intuition is more powerful than any of us can understand.

Spiritual awakening

A spiritual awakening can be an amazing experience. I learned about them through the Alcoholics Anonymous' 12-step program. Obviously, this does not mean you need to abuse substances to achieve a spiritual awakening. You can have one when you have hit rock bottom and reached a crossroads in your life. At this time, you need to choose which path to take: the one of evil that left you at rock bottom, or the one of glory, where you lift yourself back up and start growing as a person.

Spirituality means acknowledging a higher power. If you have a certain religion with its own views, you can seek enlightenment through its practices. An awakening is not necessarily religious, but it is spiritual. You can find God in surrendering yourself when you are at the lowest point in your life, but this does not mean finding it at a sacred religious place.

I am an Orthodox Christian who attends church regularly, but I didn't find God in a church. I found God while I was suffering, at a park, completely lost. I surrendered to Him. I let go and allowed God to direct my path. I follow him and am obedient towards whatever comes my way, good or bad. I know I have control over nothing, and He will fight my battles for me. I use my free will to choose His path so I can be graced with a fulfilling life.

Whatever religion or spirituality you believe in, it's all about seeking enlightenment beyond what we understand. It's about that gut feeling you get from knowing and accepting. When you confront your past that landed you at rock bottom, it wakes you up and makes you more present. You can recognize life for what it really is and gain the inner peace you've longed for instead of walking around blindly, lost and confused.

You become a new person. The old you doesn't make sense now that you know material wealth, social status, and ego-driven desires are not the answer. When you chase things like this that have no meaning, you remain trapped in a void of emptiness. This is when you transform into a unique free thinker with complete inner peace. When you realize that there is more to life than what the mediocre chase, you direct yourself toward your purpose. The fear and confusion you always had about not knowing what you were doing in life are gone. You woke up and found the answer to your destiny.

Spiritual awakenings can be difficult to cope with at first, as you have just reached a turning point in your life. You're finally connecting all the dots in your life and realizing everything has happened for a reason; it wasn't just a coincidence.

If you experience a spiritual awakening, don't be afraid. Endure through it and come out with a new and improved perspective on life and the world.

The limits of logic and the call to the spiritual

Intuitive thinking is far beyond explanation; it is what you feel very deep inside that seems to connect with everything in your life. The universe shows you your calling in a way you simply cannot explain to anyone. It's something you know without even thinking about it. In fact, it's almost like a gift you possess in the same way Mozart wrote masterpieces, or how Einstein's remarkable work in physics led him to become one of the most influential people in the 20th century.

Intuition exceeds the limits of logic. Imagine you have such a gift for writing that you can effortlessly write 10,000 words in a week, while educated people struggle to write 500 words. Nothing can explain your gift; you just do it intuitively without conscious thought. This is the spiritual realm communicating through your intuition. It comes from a place beyond human understanding, so what other answer could there be?

The truth is not always explained; sometimes it is felt. How? Your feelings give you the answer without logic entering the equation, bringing you inner peace. Then you take action using the truth you uncovered to create your masterpiece from an abstract concept. Eventually, you build something grand and successful that the world sees. People will ask, "How did you do it?" You'll say it was intuition; that it just felt right. In fact, you just went along with it—and it actually worked out after all your effort. It all made sense without any explanation.

It's incredible when you realize fully-formed concepts can just come to you without any conscious thought. You can work through all the steps with logic, but you already know it's going to work regardless. The world is beyond our control when it comes to whether our concept is recognized. That's how people give up and why the greatest inventions are never released—they remain abstract, half-done physically, or completed but abandoned because the person doubted themselves and stopped believing in their work.

There is an interesting contrast between the rational mind and our intuition. The rational mind makes sense of everything when we go through the process of solving a problem. With our intuition, on the other hand, we already know in our gut how to solve the problem. The belief is so strong, yet we can't explain precisely how we're certain it will work. It's a spiritual experience that we have to acknowledge and accept from the grace we've received.

When spiritual callings come into your life, make sure you acknowledge them. They are blessings from God or whichever deity you believe in, gifting you with a purpose to fulfill, and tailored for you.

Living from spiritual intuition

When you become a spiritual person after your awakening, life will be very different, but more fulfilling. You no longer lack a sense of belonging. There are many spiritual people out there who have been through the same process and continue to live their lives spiritually, channelling their intuition more often than those who haven't followed this path of enlightenment.

The confidence that comes with living with spiritual intuition is incredible. Going through ego death and finding yourself at one with the universe. You become less insecure. This is especially true when it comes to people you have always longed to impress. You may have sought their approval to boost your self-esteem and get a quick hit of dopamine from a false compliment. Now that you know yourself, you know that you are enough. If people don't see that, you have every reason to eject them from your life. You are perfect in your imperfections. Others will see the confidence you have in yourself, and you will become a magnetic person. You don't care about what others think of you, so you do not need validation. You're simply living your best life, and people vibe with that energy.

There will be more enjoyment of the little things, too. People look up at the night sky, but they can't appreciate its beauty. They sit there for two minutes before they get bored from a lack of stimulation. A spiritual person could sit there for an hour, staring in awe at the dark atmosphere, with the stars and moon illuminating it, and appreciating how vast it is. It puts into perspective how small we are and allows us to accept that we are just a speck of dust in a grand universe. The stillness is calming, and simple moments like this can be very powerful. Remember that intuition gets to work when your mind is at ease.

Make spirituality practical by creatively expressing intuitive thoughts through your passions. If you are skilled in the arts, use your wide imagination to create your masterpiece. Being spiritual helps enormously with creativity. Using your creativity nourishes your soul, which in turn fuels your intuitive thinking, allowing you to come up with more brilliant ideas, as if by magic. This chain reaction of momentum in your creativity keeps you inspired, allowing you to flow in a direction where your work becomes more competent through your consistent practices. Don't you think that is incredible?

When you aren't afraid to delve into the unknown, you explore more of it. You'll notice more ideas gradually surfacing in your mind. Seeing life through the eyes of the extraordinary doesn't make you crazy; the world may not understand your personal, unique experience of being spiritually awake, but it brings a life of abundance.

The nature of inner knowing

Believing in a higher power ignites your soul in a way that guides you to discover your purpose. If you have faith and stick by it, everything starts to make sense, but only you will fully understand this experience. That's the beauty of going beyond logical reasoning; you simply understand, especially when you've been lost for years with no direction. When you start building quality habits, you'll fix your life, and your purpose will suddenly come to you. Spend time incorporating your intuitive thinking to gain enlightenment.

When the unexplainable has been explained to you through a feeling from the spirit, don't overthink what is happening, and don't be afraid. Go through it and follow that path. When a higher power shows you signs, and you pick them up through your intuition, this is a calling. It's a very powerful and meaningful one that you must take into consideration. Let it guide you along the path less traveled so you can work hard on your purpose. When you choose to be faithful to your intuition, you reap the rewards you sowed when you chose to believe that the unknown is making itself known.

When you follow your calling and see it work out, you know it's true. It's all happening to you, and you've seen it intuitively. Understanding this and seeking to maintain that inner awareness becomes very beneficial for living the best quality of life.

What's great about this inner knowing is that it precedes our reasoning. When you're meditating on a thought, pondering its meaning, your intuitive thinking comes into play. When you search deep into your current thoughts and realize you've experienced them before, but never understood them, suddenly it all becomes clear. You may have reflected on it in the past, but somehow missed all the steps to get to the answer you now have. Now that your intuition has given you the answer, you can work backward and find a rational explanation for it.

Don't confuse intuition and wishful thinking. Intuition gives you answers that point you in the right direction. True inner knowing has a calm confidence. You just agree with it. There is no need to convince yourself to follow a certain path because you believe it will work. You just know it's what you have to do, and there is no stopping you. On the other hand, wishful thinking is an empty desire that you pursue desperately, although most of the time, it never materializes. If it does, you may feel empty upon realizing it is meaningless because it is not part of your calling. So, take a step back from wishful thinking. Don't pursue things that aren't part of your own personal plan, and have the faith to follow your purpose granted to you from a higher power.

Trusting yourself when there's no proof

It can be challenging to trust yourself when external noise is coming from everywhere. Not only does it distract you from thinking clearly, but it can also be tempting to seek external approval; however, this assumes that others are right without even trying to find the answers yourself. To trust when there is no truth is to have the confidence to do what you believe is right anyway, no matter what others say. If Steve Jobs hadn't followed his intuition when creating all of Apple's revolutionary products over several decades, the world would be a very different place. Someone else may have had Steve's mindset for making revolutionary products.

When you follow signals from a higher power, it's very important to put trust in yourself and in the divine. There is a reason behind everything you have seen, done, and plan to do. So, do it all without fear of being wrong, as you will inevitably be wrong at different parts of the journey, but your trust in your intuitive thinking will drive you to keep going.

Steve Jobs is living proof of the strength in believing in both a higher power and himself. It paid off tremendously for him and left a mark on this planet that few people can compare to.

When your intuition gives you a push toward the answer you're looking for, trust that your instincts will get you where you're trying to go. This will help you build trust in yourself. For example, if you're innovating a new product, starting a business, or revolutionizing your mindset through fitness, these build momentum when your intuition provides real results through action. You begin to trust yourself even more, strengthening your faith that all is going according to plan.

The amazing part is that you know this will work. You just need to put in the effort to make it into something life-changing. The road is not easy, but you must never give up when you know how well it could do. The choice is yours whether you endure all the way through the ups and downs of the journey ahead. Having belief and faith doesn't guarantee immediate results, so don't expect it. Trust the process and trust your gut feeling will eventually work things out if you don't take any shortcuts and continue to work hard until you get to the finish line.

Your faith in yourself and your cognizance of your purpose will keep you from holding yourself back in life. This is special. In fact, most people don't have this kind of intuition. So when the answer comes without explanation, even if it's just a feeling of knowing, go towards it. Don't run. Your trust in yourself and your intuition will grow stronger the more you work on it.

The battle between head and heart

There is often conflict between logic and intuition; a tension between following your head and following your heart and gut. The real key is balancing the use of both, but when it comes to making important decisions, you need to learn when to follow each. Rational thought is effective at breaking down the issue and developing a solution. Sometimes, however, logic won't suffice, and instead the answer comes to us from a feeling, and the reasoning comes afterwards. Rather than going through the process of analyzing the problem, forming a hypothesis, and testing it—which all come from our head—our intuition tells us otherwise. We might find the same answer via a different path, but without the need to work for it. We may even find a better answer that conflicts with what our head tells us.

Our belief and faith lie in our gut and heart rather than our head; that's why we get the answer instantly and without hesitation. When we doubt ourselves, we are forced to think more logically to find the answer. We need to prove it's right so we can be assured we have found the answer. It sounds intense, but this is exactly how the conflict works.

Personally, I love intuition when it shows its amazing benefits. Logic can be overbearing if you don't use it correctly. When you look too far into something and become obsessed with finding the right answer, you're overthinking it. That will only lead to you burning out and abandoning your goal. If you take the time to remain calm, your intuition will start working for you, providing you with a clear sense of direction. As a bonus, this state of calm leads us to consistent productivity. The more we take action, the more results we'll get. Each action will bring us a step closer to accomplishing the goal.

When your head is overwhelmed, turn to your heart and gut. However, when emotion overwhelms you, turn to your head. It's up to you to decide which type of thinking to channel in the moment. Just remember to maintain the balance between them so you don't become too somber or too buried in your feelings. Balance is crucial.

The body will signal to you when your intuition has something to say. When your body is tight and uncomfortable, you know something is wrong, regardless of the situation. When your body is relaxed, and you feel a sense of openness, your inner knowing tells you that you're in a safe place. Intuitive thinking helps that sense of knowing preceding logic; that is, when you develop rational thoughts about your present situation.

Living with belief and faith in a rational world

Living with belief means standing for something and having faith in a cause you trust to be true. You become a fighter, standing up for your beliefs. No matter what battles arise, you stand your ground and prove to others that your beliefs are valuable and worthy of recognition, not only to you, but to others.

This is how a movement can begin. It doesn't mean manipulating people or being destructive. It can be a cultural movement you are building to help others grow alongside you, such as a clothing line with a peaceful message of freedom as its main theme.

People who stay true to their beliefs hold on to their inner faith, even when others are skeptical or cynical, telling them how they're wrong. People may even put pressure on you to let go of your beliefs, seeing them as irrational because they can't see your vision. Even the people closest to you may doubt your vision. Don't feel discouraged; they may have healthy doubts because they care for you, even if they can't see the brilliance behind your vision. Others may doubt you for bad intentions; these people aren't worth paying attention to. They are jealous because they cannot take action in their own lives to achieve their visions. They lack your inner knowing.

Consider Conor McGregor and his unwavering belief in his ability to become a world champion in the Ultimate Fighting Championship MMA. Throughout the prime of his career, he predicted which fights he would win. His predictions would become reality, and he won every fight leading up to the title fight.

Before fighting for the belt against Jose Aldo, McGregor predicted a first-round knockout. Many people didn't believe him, assuming he was overconfident and that the dominating fighter would pick him apart. If you look at the press conferences before the fight, you can see in McGregor's aura that, in his mind, he had already won. He was intimidating Aldo with mind games. Once the fight began, he knocked Aldo out in under a minute—one of the most spectacular sporting moments in history.

McGregor declared it to the entire world before it even happened. His belief in himself was incredible. The doubters saw how irrational he was, as no one had beaten Aldo in around a decade. Aldo had won multiple title fights against other skilled challengers. McGregor proved to all the doubters that he was the true champion at the time.

That's how it needs to be for all of us. When the world doesn't see it, that's okay—you see your capabilities to succeed in whatever your purpose is.

Living intuitively–integrating intuition into daily life and decisions

Using your intuitive thinking daily can help you make quick decisions–ones you already know will help you be more productive, whether that be at work, at home, or out in public. Everyone should make intuitive thinking a habit. While you may prefer to use it only in important moments to make the right decisions or find stillness, daily practice will benefit you. When a more crucial situation arises, you will be more able to exercise your intuition because the habits you've built have taught you to use it more wisely.

Intuition can guide us in the important aspects of our lives, such as our relationships, creativity, and career choices. Imagine meeting the love of your life for the first time. You catch each other's eye and make an instant connection. You know you have a fondness for each other with just a glance. You make a move, nervous about making a good first impression.

As you talk, your intuition will give you signals about how it's going. Your brain is subconsciously cataloguing everything: body language, tone of voice, and emotional energy. You sense there is interest, but you're not getting a definitive answer. This could lead to something magical—an everlasting love you recognized through intuitive thinking.

Our creativity, when using our intuition, can spark a turning point. It's that wonderful vibration you feel in the gut when you are halfway through a project but get stuck on the next step. It's finding that stillness so you can focus on how to move forward with the best results. These signals that run through your body help you understand how to get unstuck. The focus is on seeing how we can move forward and get an answer. You're making progress, and your confidence and momentum are at a high level. When logic is blocked by a mental road hump, our intuition provides the stillness necessary to exercise our creativity. This is how a free thinker excels: they know how to exercise their thoughts strategically. When logic doesn't help, they use the predecessor: intuition.

Very intuitive people tend to live differently. Free thinkers are more aligned with their purpose. We see how all the dots connect and how it works out in our favor when building our empire. We make spontaneous decisions, whether big or small. The calculated risks taken from these decisions are always worth it, as they make life more entertaining.

Use this type of thinking, and you'll start to see the extraordinary in the ordinary.

Part IV

Living as a Free Thinker

Helping Others – How Contributing to Others' Lives Sharpens Your Own Thinking

The practical power of contribution

Contributing to society is a valuable practice that more people need to embrace.

How?

We can support individuals working to improve their lives or resist oppression in their communities. We can stand up for others humbly, doing our duty to make the world a little more peaceful. We should always do our best to be compassionate towards others and show empathy. And we can back people who struggle to stand on their own two feet.

This is such a rewarding mindset to have. The world needs more people who help one another. In many societies, people often prioritize their own interests, lacking the open-mindedness to think practically and help their neighbors, but this is not what being human is about. All of us are on this journey together, and although we're technically alone as individuals, it feels amazing to know we don't need to feel lonely; someone out there will care and help us out.

A practical way to contribute to others is to give advice. Use the wisdom you have built up over years of a life of abundant experiences, both difficulties and successes, to help others when they ask for it. If you share the knowledge you've learned, your experiences can turn into valuable information.

When people mentor in this way, those they are helping can come up with their own solutions to overcome their obstacles. It's an amazing feeling, and very rewarding, as a mentor, to see someone else rise, particularly when they've used your advice to solve their problem. A simple piece of advice can help elevate someone's life.

Helping others is a form of charity that gives you a better perspective on life. It exposes you to the real-world realities of people's lives. For example, volunteering at a homeless shelter in the winter allows you to see how the less fortunate struggle to access basic necessities like a meal, a shower, and a warm place to sleep, and you'll realize how the smallest offerings can help someone survive another night.

Volunteering shows your compassion for helping the less fortunate and fosters a deeper appreciation for life, especially when you are more fortunate, with a roof over your head, with access to warm meals, and clean water.

Helping the less fortunate doesn't only benefit them; it also gives you the drive to keep striving in your life, as there is meaning in pursuing your purpose. A big part of this is giving back, no matter how successful you become.

Life isn't always about you. It's time to shift your focus from yourself to giving back to those in need. Whether that means volunteering, mentoring, or forming a team in your business where everyone rises together, not just you. Whatever it is, just do something for someone else.

Empathy–the bridge to clearer thinking

Empathy can be difficult for people to grasp. When other people are struggling, you may be caring for their needs and sharing your energy with them. But when you're struggling and signal how you feel, no one seems to reciprocate. It's a hard pill to swallow, as this has happened to all of us at least once.

If you've never helped another, I worry about the sort of person you are. But if you need help and nobody offers, it can feel like no one cares about your problems. People do care. Some of the people you go to may still be hiding demons they are battling, not realizing they should be empathetic towards you as well. Some try to keep their energy for themselves, not always with bad intentions. Don't worry, just stay humble and true to yourself.

If you hate the world for making you feel like no one cares, look at it this way: the world doesn't owe you anything. This is why most people don't express empathy and remain narcissistic. No one has ever reached out and given them a helping hand. If this is you, and you really can't see anyone reaching out, then go out and start doing good deeds during your struggles. Keep doing it, and watch everything fall into place.

Being compassionate when you are drowning in misery is one of the toughest things to do, but it builds you up so high. It shows how strong and brave a person you are. No one helped you when you were struggling, but you made it through. Life will reward you so much more because your experiences foster humility.

If you can think practically when your mind is clouded and still succeed, I have the utmost respect for you. Few people take part in these acts of kindness. I guarantee life will flourish for you, in God's time.

In an emergency, being empathetic could save someone's life. If someone is going through a hard time, they could be on the brink of a breakdown. We have no choice but to think practically by being empathetic towards them so they can calm down, and work with them to solve the problem they are facing. Give them support, advice, and comfort. Care for their needs in times of distress. It's our human duty to be there for others in times like this.

If you want to be the hero of the story, don't turn a blind eye to these situations because you think you cannot handle the pressure. I consider this to be the wrong approach. Pressure can come at any time in our lives, so we need to learn to handle it wisely. Empathy should be viewed as a remedy for distress that helps us remain calm.

Solving real problems through service

It requires a practical thinker to help solve issues in a community, whether they be political, social, or environmental. Everyone has their own beliefs about the rural areas they should help and want to see change in, making a difference to help everyone live together in better harmony.

A starting point for giving the cause greater meaning is prioritizing community benefit over self-gain. If we view it as a win for the community, not just ourselves, we recognize that the community is the winner regardless of the outcome. When we gather as a community and work as a team, we move from abstract thinking to action to get the win. This is how we achieve real solutions together.

The most genuine reason to help is to uplift others, not just for personal benefit. Being self-reliant is amazing, but it's easier with support. It's when we work together that we learn cooperation and teamwork, and when we unite people, this awareness will spread.

Become a known figure in your community; don't hide in the crowd.

When it comes to real-world issues, staying focused on finding solutions helps you assist others more effectively. When someone asks for your help, this means they must be stuck, unable to find a solution to the situation they are dealing with, so extend your hand. You have distance from the problem, meaning you're able to think clearly compared to the person who is stressed about the issue they can't solve. It's up to you to maintain focus and view the situation from an outsider's perspective.

Imagine your friend is having trouble with dating. He wants to find a partner and get married eventually. He keeps talking to different women on dating apps, but it's not going anywhere. He's getting desperate, and this is when he asks for your advice: "How should I approach this situation better?"

You might say, "You're rushing to find someone, which is causing you to panic. Trying to find a woman as soon as possible by talking to different women each week isn't working—no one sticks around. My advice is to stop overthinking it, focus your energy on yourself, and stop wasting time talking to so many prospects. Start a journey of self-care, build self-respect, and work on yourself and your purpose. Women will notice, and one day, someone will catch your eye. It happens naturally, not when you constantly look. Stop putting finding a partner as soon as possible on a pedestal. Trust the process by putting yourself first, and then someone will come."

When we provide advice to others and solve real problems plaguing communities, we transform passive knowledge into active wisdom.

The feedback loop of growth

The more you contribute to others, the more capable you become in helping them solve problems; each experience makes you more competent in handling situations.

People will respect you more for being helpful and praise you for showing them loyalty. It's the type of feedback we deserve. Helping others can be challenging, but it can also be very rewarding.

Helping others and serving their needs gives life meaning. It makes life worth living more than being selfish; a meaningful life gives us the perspective to become better free thinkers.

Let's take a look at Tom's story to see how this all works:

Since Tom was a child, buildings and their construction have fascinated him, especially when he drove past job sites. From an early age, Tom knew his purpose was to be a property developer. Continuing through high school, Tom developed a keen sense of economics and finance, which further solidified his purpose of building. As he became older, he embarked on a tremendous career in the industry, becoming a successful developer in his forties and amassing considerable financial wealth. Tom's purpose was driven by his passion for the industry, which was rewarded with financial gain and a lasting impact, ultimately making him a prominent figure.

Tom's biggest reward was his compassion for helping others through his business, which created its own little economy. His projects have provided jobs, helping families afford food. He sells his properties to investors seeking future profits, allowing them to grow their wealth.

As Tom succeeded in his purpose, he also thought practically about how he could help others and how they could work as a team. This feedback loop led to growth for everyone who worked hard and smart in Tom's empire; this is how real businessman should carry out their duties.

Being a brilliant, free-thinking person who continues to help others transforms our passive knowledge into active wisdom, enabling us to share valuable insights with those who need our guidance. Wisdom can captivate when conveyed through powerful words with meaning behind them, rather than empty information you don't believe. Understand their underlying issues. Feel and really resonate with what the other person is going through, so you can channel your wisdom and share it with the person seeking it. Make sure you pay attention; don't be someone who doesn't care about others' problems.

Being helpful makes things easier, but even in tough situations, you know what to say about common issues. Wisdom is a gift earned through overcoming struggles; so be grateful.

Always make sure helping others is part of your purpose. If your purpose is to build an empire, do it for the sake of humanity.

Kindness

Kindness as a choice, not weakness

Being a true independent thinker means recognizing that kindness is not weakness. In fact, it's the complete opposite.

The world portrays kindness as submission and treats people who express it as soft and spineless. Blinded by greed and pride, our society believes powerful people dominate, and that agenda is best established through force. However, while this may work initially, those who follow this rule will eventually pay for their wickedness, and when they suffer the consequences, no one will listen to their pleas for help.

Acts of kindness maintain our inner peace when we find ourselves in a heated argument. We don't feel the need to match someone else's poor behavior. Being kind to someone aggressive does not mean we are being submissive. We don't need to tolerate their bad attitude, as that would also mean stooping down to their level. Acting with kindness requires more strength than most people comprehend.

Bystanders who witness an argument may perceive the reactive person as the dominant one due to their ferocious tone and aggressive actions. Ignorant people may see us as weak, but we should remain grounded and in control, refusing to descend to the level of an angry fool. The real test of strength is our ability to handle pressure when someone is in our face like this. We can still defend ourselves, but it's crucial to de-escalate the situation and avoid unnecessary confrontations, while keeping ourselves out of harm's way.

Eventually, bystanders will realize we were the stronger person, and the reactive person was the weak one. We can see it as using our kindness to de-escalate the situation by controlling their energy and calming them down, but it's for a genuine reason. The goal is to use our kindness to gradually calm them down.

Independent thinkers can choose to be kind without being perceived as weak. This is remarkable because, while others may still see kindness as weak, independent thinkers can uphold their principles and defend what's right, regardless.

Never let others pressure you into reacting a certain way when a situation escalates. Treat them with kindness to prevent the issue from escalating.

Be kind, not nice

As a general rule, people want to be liked and avoid conflict, but this can result in being 'too nice', which is often seen as submissive behavior. The thing to remember here is that we don't earn respect by trying to please people. In fact, others will only try to exploit our desperation for their own gain.

If we want to be liked, don't be 'nice'. Seeking validation signals to others that we aren't comfortable with ourselves. Instead, we can engage in self-love by prioritizing our needs over others as if we are the only person who exists. An independent thinker will accept their own faults when they recognize their longing for validation; in other words, we become independent through self-acceptance. There is no higher value than being free from a conforming world filled with selfish pride.

When we fully accept ourselves, people will notice us. We may not realize it at first, but over time, the people around us will come to accept us and openly show respect. We must then respond with kindness.

Kindness inspires authentic concern for others. This can sometimes be hard for an independent thinker, but it's important to remember that acts of kindness aren't about seeking praise but about doing something genuinely good. Imagine a friend you love is going through something tough. You respond with desperation, acting to make yourself feel better. You don't consider how your energy is impacting your friend, and don't realize your actions, which essentially equate to being 'in your friend's face', are only piling more stress on your friend.

A kind person, on the other hand, can show support in a similar situation by genuinely listening and being there for the other person. For example, you might assist your friend by cleaning their house while they stay in bed.

Another key difference between being kind and being nice is the need for gratitude. Kind people don't seek gratitude, but nice people will keep bringing up what they've done in an attempt to gain approval. This need for gratitude only makes things worse for the person who is struggling. A kind person, however, will continue to fulfill their duties, even in the absence of gratitude, because they know it will make their loved one feel more at ease.

It's not harmful to be a little submissive in the right circumstances, such as when people (like family members and close friends) cannot take advantage of you. But if you make a habit of being submissive, people will notice and lose respect for you. Negativity gathers around overly nice people, leaving them vulnerable to being taken advantage of.

Basically, act with kindness and stop being so nice.

Good guys don't come last, but the nice ones do. A good guy is a man of kindness; a nice man is submissive and lets people get their way when they are in the wrong.

Real-world kindness as quiet rebellion

Real-world kindness means setting an example through your courage and teaching others to follow in your footsteps.

Even in the small moments, we can be a person of value. It's the small, inconsequential offerings that denote real-world kindness, like assisting an older person across the road, aiding someone who has fallen, or soothing a visibly upset stranger.

Genuine kindness, when you expect nothing in return, demonstrates humility and the absence of self-aggrandisement. When you express gratitude or react to someone, people around you notice these small signals, which, in turn, significantly influence how they perceive your grace and prompt them to wonder whether they have the same discipline.

If they know they don't, your actions may inspire them to clean up their own act. When you show that you don't need validation for your acts of kindness, it encourages others to examine their own behaviors.

It is hard to think independently in this way, but keeping up these acts of kindness every day will make you a stronger and more faithful person. When you start doing the right things, your mindset growth can be unbelievable.

The real power moves often occur in cruel, ego-driven environments. For example, charity functions are often attended by prominent people in high society. While we may think they are there to support charity, if we watch closely, we may realize that many are there more for the opportunity to network with other high society members. We'll notice that they talk to each other, flattering one another, while also keeping an eye out for the person with the biggest presence at the event. Their actions demonstrate an ulterior motive.

Imagine you are part of that society; a well-established person who has worked hard to achieve your current status. If you know how these wealthy entrepreneurs act, but refuse to play their game, then you can call yourself a true independent thinker. To do this, you may engage in minor acts of kindness to disrupt the environment of greedy, money-hungry men and women. This is not difficult. Your acts of kindness at the venue could be as simple as genuinely wishing people well, being polite to waiters who look unhappy on their shift, or helping set up before the evening starts. Other attendees will notice and be unsure what to think; they see a successful person who, unlike the rest of the attendees, is also humble, and this disrupts their environment.

Ego-driven individuals often feel they have been put on display to make up for the fact that they haven't helped out. It's like they are trying to cover it up. They may not admit it, but they certainly think about it. Being a disrupter means placing a small seed of doubt in someone's mind, something that leads them to become fixated on questioning why you are so kind.

Disrupt your environment with such confidence that people are left in shock. Most people work with their ego, so when you work with kindness at a prominent level without expecting anything in return, it's intimidating to people. It sets an example for how true leaders should act.

Be kind to yourself

As an independent thinker, it's very important to regularly practice kindness toward yourself, as well as toward others.

When you are kind, grateful, and loving to yourself, rather than bitter, life becomes worth living.

Being kind to yourself means rewarding yourself. Treat yourself according to your preferences: gifts, clothes-shopping, holiday trips. Do whatever lights your candle. Everyone deserves happiness, especially those with moral character, as life can be stressful.

However, do remember that while it's good to reward yourself, it's not good to overindulge. If fashion is your thing and you earn enough to splurge on clothes you want, then by all means, buy them. If you like electronics, consider buying a new phone or laptop that can elevate your work and give you something new to play with. But don't go over the top. Only buy what you need and will use.

My personal favorite way to treat myself is to go on a holiday. This is a great way to unwind if you can find the opportunity. Once you book a trip, you can look forward to visiting your dream destination, letting your hair down, and meeting strangers who could become lifelong friends. The excitement that builds in the present moment is the best feeling and the ultimate reward.

Being kind to ourselves means acknowledging that we deserve a worthwhile life. We work hard, but when we get a break, we should make the most of it. Go out and do things you want to do. When you have spare time, make the most of it. If you enjoy activities like golf, bowling, or socializing at cafes with friends, do them! Enjoy your life and have some fun, because life is too short to be taken too seriously. The moments go by quickly, so make time for activities that bring you happiness.

Working on our dreams, goals, and purpose is the most important part of being human. It is essential that we follow our calling; however, it's important to remember that we have a life outside of our work. That's why entertainment exists. It's there for our pleasure.

We're all deserving of kindness. Life passes by quickly, and if we don't take the opportunity to be silly and playful, we'll miss out on so many spontaneous moments—and believe me, they matter. Fun isn't just for kids; they might indulge in it more easily than adults, but adults are just as capable of taking a break, being kind to themselves, and enjoying some of their personal healthy pleasures.

Let Go of Distractions – Stay Focused

The age of distraction–why focus is rare and valuable

Focus keeps the winners ahead, while distraction holds the losers back. Few people focus, as most prefer to distract themselves because it's easier.

Most people choose diversions to escape discomfort and boredom. They procrastinate and delay necessary tasks, leaving them trapped in a cycle of distraction and inaction. If you're in this situation, you need to minimize distractions so you can complete the important tasks. Start by focusing on positive hobbies that stimulate your brain and combat boredom.

Whether you like to play chess, have coffee with a friend, or take your dog for a walk, as long as it's positive, it will callous your brain, helping you build momentum and continue living a life of focus. This will drive you to tackle important things, rather than putting them on the back burner out of laziness and unhealthy habits.

Developing a healthy obsession with activities that give you a dopamine hit is a game-changer if you want to become more focused and driven. One of my personal favorites is hot and cold therapy. This therapy involves spending some time in the sauna in hot conditions, then getting out and jumping straight into an ice bath in freezing weather. I'll be honest: it sucks. But when it's over, the clarity you gain is phenomenal. You leave with a clear mind, ready to focus on the tasks you need to accomplish.

Sitting at home, idly watching movies, not only doesn't get your body moving, but it does nothing for your focus. Activity sharpens focus. Even getting a massage, once a week, to loosen your tense muscles, will help you relax and feel ready to take action and work on your life goals.

Most people remain stuck in unhealthy dopamine patterns that distract them from striving for more. Digital overstimulation, for example, reduces our attention span, keeping us in a state of constant scrolling. We can become stuck in a cycle of irrelevant information, as we seek out pointless entertainment and read negative comments on posts that just make us angry. We know we'll just get angry before we pull out our phones, but we still do it!

Individuals with an addiction to doom scrolling need to curtail their unhealthy social media consumption. This is especially true for the so-called popular people who are hit with a constant barrage of notifications and always feel the need to reply. Their attention is repeatedly stolen throughout the day, distracting them and leaving no time to complete meaningful and important tasks.

The ability to focus for extended periods of time is highly valuable. It puts us miles ahead of most people. It's time to face the truth and start utilizing dopamine in a healthy way.

Identifying what truly matters–defining your priorities

Think about what's going on when you share your goals with people. Are they what you really want to accomplish in life? Or are you just saying them because they sound good or because you think you have to? Have your distractions prevented you from setting your true goals and determining your true purpose?

If you answered yes to the last question, start prioritizing what truly matters so you can avoid distractions that hold you back from determining and completing your purpose. All the distractions we so love to indulge in may appear urgent because we feel we need a break, but what we're really doing is creating a time-wasting habit and reducing our attention span. These distractions shouldn't be an excuse to neglect putting time, effort, and energy into our life goals because they lack the enduring importance of our purpose and ultimately lead to nothing beyond a break, which is healthy on occasion.

What truly matters to you?

Your long-term goals, purpose, and core values are what really matter, so why do we come up with all these excuses to avoid directing our full effort and attention toward our life aspirations? We avoid hardship because we're too comfortable and lack the courage to endure the pain of failures, setbacks, and heartbreak.

The real value of the journey toward focus lies in achieving success by persevering and avoiding distractions.

If you are distracted by people who drain your energy, maybe it's time to take a step back and focus on yourself. It's difficult when you have a family, obviously, but this doesn't mean you can't take some time to focus on yourself. Not only will this elevate you, but it will also elevate your family. fulfilling your ambitions–whether they are for financial gain, to pursue a new career, or to create a happier household–benefits everyone because if you don't help yourself first, you will struggle to help others.

Take your energy back from others, especially those who are toxic. Take a break when others are sapping too much of your energy. If they persist and take it too far, realize that it's time to cut that friendship out of your life. Tell yourself that you're worth more than that, and their ignorance and manipulation are holding you back.

If your priorities seem overwhelming, take the pressure off yourself and focus on your purpose one day at a time. The plan is set; now it's time to stay focused on the present moment. It's all we have. Stop looking too far ahead; you haven't reached that point yet. It doesn't exist. All you have is now and the actions you take today that are guided by your plan.

Cutting the noise–stay disciplined to eliminate distractions

When you're motivated to achieve a goal, discipline isn't fleeting. It's a commitment that needs to be practiced daily. You won't always feel great, because everyone has bad days, but this is normal. On bad days, discipline is what keeps us determined to push through and achieve our purpose. Maintaining dispassion towards our passion helps us stay focused, eliminating the excitement that can lead to setbacks and distractions.

Discipline works to our advantage by helping us resist temptations when we need to work on something important.

A temptation is any weakness that leads us to slip back into our comfort zone. A few examples of such temptations include:

- excessive partying – detrimental as it erodes our self-control and stability.

- gossip among friends – never a good thing, as people who feed on gossip lack purpose, and thus they speak ill of those who succeed.

Avoid these people; they'll drag you down with their negativity, and you'll become like them.

- digital reliance – one of the worst weaknesses because it's so easy to access. All consumers need to adopt digital discipline by turning off notifications, putting their phones on mute and avoid looking at their screens when there is nothing there for them in the current moment.

Discipline is always accessible, but can be tough to regain once we've given in to temptation and laziness.

Start designing an environment that caters to your growth. Create a daily routine that keeps you structured and helps you avoid distractions. Following that routine can help you accomplish your daily goals by minimizing distractions when you have a task to do, whether this is work, exercise, family time, or anything else you need to accomplish.

Discipline means recalling your goals instead of giving in to what you feel right now. It means giving up instant gratification and removing distractions to focus on your life's goal and its future benefits.

One final important note: rest is fine—it's not the enemy of productivity. No one wants to burn out, and we all deserve rest with some minor distractions that ease our minds after a hard day. Just be sure you choose the right time, after you've completed your daily objectives.

You've earned your rest; keep it a habit and let your downtime work for you.

Living with intention, not reaction

Know this.... **reaction leads to distraction!**

If your environment is too intense and you let it affect you, your brain reacts with the wrong intentions, keeping you distracted from what you need to stay focused on. That's your own life, not one where you're distracted by others; we'll only react in a way that causes us to drift away from our plan.

To live a focused life, choose a lifestyle where you are locked into your passions, goals, and hard work every day. Your work will have a deeper meaning when you stay on the right track. Focusing on the right intentions every day will catapult your elevation. This practical way of thinking puts you ahead without you even noticing; you'll look back later and see how far you have come.

Focusing each day enhances your relationships. Your family will respond positively to your hard work and drive. When others—especially your children—observe your actions, they will follow your lead, and your spouse will respect you.

Your growth can inspire others to follow, as they can see your practical thinking in action, providing them with the protective and virtuous foundations you have built. It will lead to success in all areas, including financial success, allowing you to spend time with them rather than being miserable in a dead-end job that keeps you from being productive.

A life of focus allows you to live life on your own terms instead of reacting to everything that is thrown at you. A keen mind discerns what's right for a person, allowing them to see past distractions caused by minor problems and negative people. They try to drag you into their unhappy worlds even though you're striving to be your best, living the life you want and not the life others want for you.

Begin living with intentions that cater best to you, without neglecting to help others. However, when others drag you down for pursuing your own path, it's essential to keep them at arm's length for your peace of mind, so you can stay practical and grow daily.

Embrace the discomfort of focus, and endure the boredom of a period of repetitive work, so you can reach the next exciting step of achieving your life objectives. Hard work needs to be embraced, even if it's exhausting, because the goals are for a greater purpose.

Make a conscious decision to live a focused lifestyle. This lifestyle is a choice, and you must choose it daily through practical thinking.

Become Healthy – Applying Knowledge for Real-Life Benefits

Why physical wellness begins in the mind

Make the decision to follow a path towards health for a better quality of life. Be honest with yourself here: do you see people with healthy lifestyles complain about their problems dramatically, like it's the end of the world, or is that something you only see from people who are not healthy?

People with healthy lifestyles are often more positive and better adjusted. Physical fitness doesn't have to be about looking good—although it's a great feeling to be comfortable naked, rather than being overweight—just don't let your ego compete when it comes to appearance. View physical fitness as a practical way of sharpening your body to sharpen your mind, giving you more discipline, confidence, and positive energy.

Practical thinking connects knowledge to action. How we treat our bodies reflects whether we are someone who thinks about our health journey and makes choices to learn and grow. We decide to shape our bodies into a fit physique so they function better.

Unfit people see fit individuals and recognize them as practical people driven by consistency. They see the results when someone is walking around in hot weather, wearing a singlet that reveals their muscle mass, toned bodies, and high vibrations.

People know maintaining a fit body requires consistent work. A fit person radiates a go-getter image.

You need the right mindset for this journey of fitness and health: your body is a temple. To gain respect for your body, you must embrace responsibility for your health and achieving beneficial results through delayed gratification. That's the mindset we gain through this work. Simply choosing water over a soft drink, a gym workout over going to the bar, or opting for a morning run instead of sleeping in keeps us moving in the right direction. The decisions we make about continuing to pursue a quality lifestyle are formed in our minds first. The next and final step is to go out there and actually do the exercise.

Physical fitness helps us shape our body's physique. If we continue, we'll find it easier to stay determined when pursuing other goals. It's all about building habits and learning lessons along the way. Completing workout goals, such as beating personal bests, gaining muscle mass, and losing weight, teaches us to take these positive habits and apply them outside the gym.

Recognize the potential for positive change in all aspects of your life. If you're already aware of the benefits but aren't applying your practical thinking to your health and fitness journey, it's time to start now. Watch how everything will change if you stay committed. Physical exercise has the potential to bring positive change to all aspects of our lives. Stay committed to the journey, and watch how everything will change.

Move the body, move the mind

Physical fitness is a mental anchor, and the importance of regular exercise is self-explanatory. What isn't as obvious is that moving the body creates energy, and our minds become as active as our bodies through training. Training strengthens the mind through intense workouts, channelling all the negative energy we have accumulated during the day and releasing it at the gym.

Imagine you argued with a coworker in the morning. Both of you were becoming aggressive, but you decided to let it go to avoid getting fired. However, your aggression has lingered throughout the day to the point where you want to put a hole through the office wall. At the end of the day, after you've clocked out, you're still in a bad mood. Now is the time to hit the gym to release all that negative energy. You enjoy resistance weight training, so you engage in an intense strength workout, releasing tension. At the end of the workout, you're exhausted, but you feel much better having channelled your anger into a positive workout. Instead of hitting your coworker or going home and getting angry with a family member, you can now leave your frustrations behind at the gym.

Physical exercise is the remedy for guiding our mental health out of darkness and back toward the light.

Movement sharpens your mind when your body is active during a workout. Our brain function increases with the heightened activity as our body flows through well-paced movements. This helps the brain improve focus and reduce stress. Exercising at the gym clears your mind and allows you to focus on things that matter for the rest of the day.

Everyone has their own preference for physical exercise. When you start your journey, ease into it and gradually build up the intensity. I won't go into detail about the vast range of exercises available to you, but briefly, here are different categories of physical exercises you can start with:

- ▹ cardiovascular exercise (brisk walks, jogging, stair climbs on a stair master machine, and cycling)
- ▹ resistance training (free weights, cable and machine training, callisthenics, bodyweight training, resistance bands, and isometric training)
- ▹ flexibility exercises (static stretching, yoga, and dynamic stretching).

Choose whichever type of exercise you desire and start making your sessions work for you. Go and do it. If you have a fully functioning body and brain, then you have no excuse. Stop being lazy and use practical thinking to live a practical life.

Eating to think, feel, and perform better

Hippocrates said: *Let food be thy medicine and medicine be thy food.* And he was right—you are what you absorb.

The better the quality of food you eat, the better the quality of your life. The lower the quality of the food you eat, the more issues arise, and the lower your quality of life. It makes a big difference; high-quality, nutritious food is the fuel for an active lifestyle that provides us with a positive outlook. Having food on the table is our biggest blessing—it provides us with the means to survive and live another day.

Many people in third-world countries don't have the same access to good food as we do in first-world countries. Most of us make a conscious decision to eat poorly, even though others would love to have the luxury of eating food with proper nutrition. Choosing easily-made and tasty processed foods is the lazy way out, and it's disappointing when people consume them to the point of addiction.

A nutritious, gut-healthy diet acts as fuel for mental clarity, focus, and lasting energy throughout the day. If you fill yourself with amazing whole foods that nourish your body, you'll likely find you don't need to consume coffee and unnatural energy drinks to the point of excess—or at all. The nutritious food we consume provides the energy we need to sustain ourselves and live our days to their fullest potential. If you find this hard to believe, try eating whole foods for yourself.

To repair your gut with a well-balanced diet, gradually reduce your intake of refined sugar and caffeine. These short-term energy boosts will only lead to a crash after an hour or two, forcing you to keep drinking more to sustain your energy levels. When your gut starts to repair itself and function better through regular clean eating, those energy crashes will be a thing of the past; you'll have a steady flow of energy that keeps you going.

Think practically and learn about diets and meal plans. Discover how different food sources work with the body to provide healthy biology, and play different roles with the nutrients they provide.

Learn how to meal plan. Cook once a week and put different meals—breakfast, lunch, snacks, and dinner—in the freezer so you can save time during your day and still have a meal filled with healthy goodness. You only need to heat it up. Doing this allows you to structure your time during the week without the need to cook all the time.

Figuring out which foods energise you and which deplete you is easy most of the time; we know what is healthy and what is not. Start eating whole foods over processed foods. Maintain a balanced intake of macronutrients, including proteins, carbs, and fats, along with healthy proteins like chicken, eggs, lean beef, and chickpeas. Healthy carbs include sweet potatoes, quinoa, oats, and brown rice. Healthy fats include avocado, Brazil nuts, and salmon. Then we have whole foods with amazing fiber, like lentils, black beans, bananas, and broccoli.

Lastly, there are probiotics, including kefir, kimchi, and sauerkraut. If you eat these food sources and many more I haven't listed, your body will love you for it. That's how we begin to love ourselves.

One final note: cheat meals are okay. It's fine to spoil yourself, but keep it to a minimum. Don't overindulge because you're tired of eating whole foods.

Schedule your treat for a certain day and enjoy it then, but don't do it every day.

Health as a way of life–integration, consistency, and long-term thinking

Health is a way of life. Ask how you would like to see yourself in the long term. Would you like to be an active, outgoing, and adventurous person who achieves their health goals and elevates their life's work to massive heights of success? Or would you prefer to remain lazy, eating processed garbage, being out of shape, and never stepping out of your comfort zone to be the person you desire to be?

The key is to live a healthy lifestyle; it's a choice we make to be the best version of ourselves.

People fail because they follow the crowd, seeing fitness as just a trend. When a content creator launches an active clothing line that sparks a movement, it might motivate you to start your health journey, but fitness is not a trend—it's a lifestyle. It's not simply about taking part in a movement everyone else follows and will eventually abandon; it's you versus you, and it's up to you to keep living this healthy lifestyle.

Trends are cool, I admit, but they only provide a small boost of inspiration. If you give up after a short while, you're not treating it as a lifestyle, and that's the difference between the winners and losers on a health journey. Don't get too caught up in trends. Go out there and live the dream of having a healthy lifestyle. Develop an outlook on life that contains more light than darkness.

A healthy lifestyle isn't just about food and exercise. You must get enough sleep because regular sleep is very important for health, recovery, and brain function. You should do it consistently. Don't be someone who stays up all night for no reason when you're capable of sleeping, but instead of getting a good rest, you play video games and only sleep for a few hours. In the morning, you'll go to work feeling very groggy. This is a terrible pattern. That's why people consume so much coffee per day; they lack a routine that ensures proper sleep.

If you struggle to maintain a healthy lifestyle, get yourself an accountability partner who is on the same journey. Holding each other accountable helps both of you accomplish your daily health goals and reach your long-term health and fitness objectives.

Find a community of fitness fanatics where everyone uplifts one other to do their best. It'll help keep you in line, as well as all who need guidance, and also for us to guide others, because iron sharpens iron.

Resilience and Adaptability – Handling Life's Challenges Effectively

Building resilience–bouncing back with strength and clarity

Bouncing back from life's challenges can seem hard, and you may feel like you aren't ready for change. That's the whole point: you can't always be ready. Sometimes you have no choice but to move forward from an uncontrollable scenario. Life keeps going, and you have to flow with it.

We should view the challenges we face as opportunities for growth. Our experiences can make or break us, and resilience is the key to bouncing back from a downfall. Imagine bouncing back like an underdog who had no chance of winning his battles. By building our self-belief, we can rise to the challenge and move on to the next chapter of our lives, experiencing the glorious victory of overcoming our struggles. It may be a rough road to overcome adversity, but making it through your hardships will turn you into a powerful person.

Resilience is your partner in overcoming and adapting; it will always have your back. Never lose belief in yourself, even when the world has become a dark place. See the light that is you. Illuminate the world by overcoming setbacks and bouncing back without letting your light burn out. If it's only a little dim, that's okay.

Those who experience hardship at a young age learn resilience early. If they manage to overcome all their traumas and setbacks when they're older, you won't find a stronger person. It's very difficult to hurt a person like this.

If a young adult has navigated tough experiences–childhood abuse, drugs, hanging out with the wrong crowd, involvement in criminal activity, jail time–and still emerged resilient as they adapt to an alternative lifestyle, they have something special.

People who've 'been there' see life for what it truly is. They've cultivated a mindset that not only avoids self-destruction but also destroys anything in its path in a positive way. People will try to put them down, but they take that energy and direct it into action to become successful. It is the best and only revenge: being successful.

Past struggles teach us grit. They teach us not to give up easily. We may keep getting knocked down, but we'll rise again with a smile on our faces. The world may see us as a bunch of weirdos, but I think we're courageous with an ability to think practically, even when we've gone through a difficult time.

Understanding resilience and adaptability

What does being resilient and learning to adapt to change really mean? It is difficult for all of us, but we must use practical thinking to accept adversity and move on with our lives. We must endure the pain and suffering that an experience has brought upon us.

Our practical thinking enables us to create new strategies that help advance our lives and perspectives positively, fostering a more optimistic outlook of what lies ahead. It allows us to do our best to move on and adapt to the changes that come.

Resilience

To be resilient is to bounce back from adversity, trauma, and failures. Something may kick us down, whether that's our environment or a declining mental state, but resilience means having the strength not to give up. If we don't have resilience and we give up, this can lead to a life of misery and an inability to move on from the past. In that direction lies a path of destruction with self-abuse from toxic substances or vices that eat away at your mind, body, and spirit. Resilience is the turning point between the road to recovery and the road to condemnation.

Choosing the right path requires resilience to bounce back from the hardships we endure.

Adaptability

Adaptability is the ability to adjust your thinking, reactions, and strategy in response to recent changes. It's the ability to continue adapting to the next chapter of your life, to keep pushing to find a new direction, no matter how much the past haunts you. Even if it takes some getting used to, if we want to live without being victims of our downfalls, we must do it.

How can you adapt to your new life after a harsh experience changes everything?

Accept what has happened, let go of the past, and focus on what you need to do to grow your mindset. You can do this.

Overcoming negative experiences through resilience and adaptation gives us a head start in becoming focused and disciplined. We can choose to see the bigger picture of why life has brought us to this point. Our traumas and failures can be the bedrock on which we mold ourselves into stronger people with character. Each tragic experience shapes us into a person of integrity, virtue, and grit if we choose the right path.

No one's life remains completely still without something unpleasant happening unexpectedly at some point. This is especially true when the unpleasant event comes from an external environment over which we have no control, such as someone close passing away, a partner leaving, or an employer suddenly going bankrupt.

Tragic adversities are beyond our control. This means that if we can't control them, we eventually need to accept and overcome them to move forward in life.

It hurts. I know this because I've felt it. However, it's part of our life journey of love, loss, friendship, betrayals, and everything in between.

Developing adaptability

The way to stay effective amid change is to choose our hell wisely.

What does this mean?

Do we choose the actual road to hell, where we remain in the same position, never learning from our mistakes, staying stuck in a moment we don't want to move on from, even though it has destroyed us and continues to put us down?

Or do we take the road that feels like hell? A path where we adapt to changes we may not want, but must accept if we wish to improve.

Be willing to make that change. Results prove you are far better off on the rollercoaster of a new journey, so growth can become a part of your mindset. Change is scary at first. You may feel lost. Your mind may race. Your emotions may heighten. This is why we must take the time to adjust, be still, continue the process, and adapt to the next phase. One day, you will suddenly realize how worthwhile it was to endure all the way to peaceful freedom.

Remain open-minded to new ideas that may give you the approach you need, whether this is the adaptability to control your emotions or the ability to make better decisions based on lessons you have learned. A positive way to adapt is to put yourself first, especially when you're around people who drain your energy. Spend that time on self-care and self-reliance, making decisions that best suit you so you can figure out which direction life will take you.

Putting yourself first is not selfish, especially when escaping your own hell; you must embrace the kindness that comes along and think practically about how it will benefit you. Moving on can be difficult, and by putting yourself first, you can adapt in a gradual, calmer way, rather than trying to force your way past, which can lead to a potential breakdown. That's not what we want.

Sometimes what we're doing isn't working, so we need to change our approach. We may cling to something familiar from the past, but if it didn't work the first few times, then we will continue to fail. We learn lessons when we keep repeating them, even if they are the wrong ones. Therefore, we must switch our strategies and take some time to experiment with them. By thinking practically, we can apply our improved approach and move forward from our adversity.

Embrace uncertainty. The unknown is nonexistent, so go with the flow and stop focusing on what isn't in your life at this very moment. You know who you are and where you want to be.

Adapting is not about abandoning our identities; rather, it's about leveraging past experiences to update our approaches and start thriving. Even if we have outgrown our friends, it's time to adapt, diversify, and make new ones.

Turning knowledge into action

If you're sitting there reading this book right now, thinking, "This guy's optimism is too unrealistic"... guess what? IT ISN'T! It is possible to apply resilience and adaptability in real life, and there are plenty of stories out there to prove it.

True underdog stories show how athletes, musicians, and actors have applied resilience and adaptability in their lives to overcome obstacles. We hear stories about how some faced mental health issues and applied resilience to bounce back from this adversity, adapting to embrace new challenges ahead, going back into their craft, putting their head down in focus, no matter how much they're hurting, and beginning their road to glory. We see them win championships, world titles, play live on a world stage, and star in A-list movies.

These stories of the underdog who everyone saw crumbling but then came back stronger are what make a story worth telling. All of us have to admire these stories, so when we fall, we know we can get back up and transform our tragedy into one of the most inspiring stories ever told.

Problems happen constantly.

Imagine losing your job suddenly after a decade of working at the same company; your long-established comfort zone has been brutally stripped away from you. You did your job well; you knew everyone, and the way the office functioned was second nature to you. When you receive the message that you've been fired, you start panicking. You're left unsure what to do next, lost in your thoughts to the point of not being able to think clearly, and you become hysterical.

You never thought about getting another job. You intended to remain at the same place until you retired; it was a part of you, and now you feel like a piece of you has died along with your job.

After sitting at home for weeks, completely lost, you finally decide to move forward and leave behind all the emotions and sadness that had taken hold of you. With money running low, you have no choice but to be resilient and bounce back from this massive change. If you don't, you could end up losing it all.

You apply for a new job similar to your old one, and they hire you. You adapt to your new work life by applying the practical thinking strategies you've acquired from your recent adversity. Adapting to the new job was difficult at first, but a year has gone by, you've settled in, and the people at the company are great to work with. You'd go so far as to say it's a healthier environment than your previous company.

You're very satisfied with your new job. You've come to realize that getting laid off wasn't the end of the world. You've seen the light at the end of the tunnel and how moving on and changing can be beneficial in the long run. Resilience and adaptability have worked together like a charm.

People who have the courage to take another shot at life and give it their best effort will be rewarded for their hard work. They'll become a practical thinker and apply resilience and adaptability to come back stronger.

Enthusiasm

The energy behind action

Enthusiasm is necessary to complete the steps toward our ultimate goal.

Enthusiasm is energy that is laser-focused on achieving your goal because you want to do it. If a goal is important to you, enthusiasm will follow. If you persevere, enthusiasm will help you stay well-balanced until you reach completion.

How do you want to live your life?

If you pursue your goals with minimal energy, only going through the motions because you told yourself you'd do this, you won't feel the genuine enthusiasm required to do your best work.

Without enthusiasm, can you say you're really interested in what you are trying to accomplish? It doesn't seem that way to me. We all have particular emotions, even those who seem not to have a heart. When you have an objective, you need to have some sort of enthusiasm to complete it.

Enthusiasm builds our momentum, boosting our energy and making us excited about our work. When you are enthusiastic, you have the energy to work efficiently, and because you enjoy the work, you get it done faster. However, beware of overexcitement, which can lead to loss of focus, and excessive emotion, which can cloud your judgment.

Although working with our passions will not always be fun, it doesn't need to be tedious; we can still find some enjoyment. When milestones are achieved or tasks are finished, celebrate those moments. This is an excellent way to maintain momentum, prevent our enthusiasm from waning, and just enjoy the journey of pursuing our dreams.

Once we reach our dream and live it, we'll realize that it's the journey itself that is amazing. By thinking practically, we can leverage enthusiasm to maintain our momentum, which plays a huge role in reaching the finish line. The spark within that won't die down keeps burning brightly, both through the good times and the bad. The work doesn't stop until you achieve a high level of success, at which point micro-managing becomes necessary to keep everything afloat. But still, we have to keep the spark aflame, no matter what.

Don't depend on your mood to keep that spark alive, however.

When things work out, we have high energy. When they're tough and boring, our mood is low. We need to maintain enthusiasm at all times, as genuine enthusiasm stems from purpose rather than emotion.

If something really matters, your mindset will stay the same, through the good times and bad, as you sincerely enjoy the ride.

How to cultivate enthusiasm (even when you don't feel it)

To cultivate enthusiasm is to keep your energy at a positive level. Life may distract us from our purpose when emergencies arise. We might have a family emergency on our hands, such as when our child falls ill at school and needs to come home, or if we fall ill ourselves and are unable to work for a week. These situations happen all the time. While they might prevent us from working on our project for a short period of time, it's only temporary. At these times, showing love and support for our families and being kind to ourselves is important.

Once you get everything sorted out, maintain the same energy toward your purpose and keep working on it every day. You haven't permanently lost momentum from being away from your work for a week. Life happens, and that's okay. Just make sure you never lose your spark so your energy levels remain high.

Surround yourself with positive people. If everyone has the right momentum when working in a team, practical thinking will naturally fall into place, leading to tremendous action and increased productivity. Ultimately, the work will get done.

If we start small, we can gradually cultivate our enthusiasm. Doing so gives us small wins that deliver little hits of excitement, encouraging us to keep working.

Respecting the process is important. We cannot know what the journey holds. By sticking to our plan, we can keep our minds focused on the present moment, knowing we're headed in the right direction. Tackling our tasks day by day allows us to progress efficiently. This is how we keep building enthusiasm, keeping that spark lit despite not knowing the outcome. Just trusting the process will lead us there.

The plan you're working toward doesn't need to have profound meaning. For example, you may be working a full-time job that's not your purpose. This is not a bad thing. Chances are you've realized what you want and need to do with your life, but just can't do it full-time currently because you have bills to pay.

Maintaining enthusiasm is important.

We may only have an hour a day to work on our dreams. If we set a goal to work on this across as many days as possible and if we commit to an hour a day, 5 days a week, then we must see it through.

Our responsibilities can take up a lot of our time, but if we make time to work on our passions, there is no excuse not to. This is how we build momentum that doesn't leave us. However, if we get lazy and months pass without any work getting done, our spark will die out. At the very least, we need to keep moving forward.

Enthusiasm without naivety

Starting a personal project without considering the downsides of over-committing can slow you down, especially when you're almost finished. Naïvety often comes from a lack of experience, knowledge, and wisdom. Be cautious when someone senses how naive you are.

If you're a trusting person who senses it, check within yourself to see if you are going too fast. You may lack a balanced mindset because you are overly enthusiastic, which leads to unrealistic expectations. Being realistic is crucial; otherwise, you will put too much energy into a project rather than pacing yourself with a focused mindset.

Being a practical thinker means being aware of this tendency toward overenthusiasm. We can become overly enthusiastic at times and rush. This can lead to burnout, so we need to be realistic to avoid falling into this trap.

Imagine you want to start a clothing line. Your enthusiasm is through the roof with the steps you're taking to launch the business: designs, marketing, and finding manufacturers. Everything is flowing smoothly, but then you become overenthusiastic and set a launch date for the following month. You don't see any problems as you're working at a high pace, eager to launch quickly, and your design meets your expectations. However, you lack marketing expertise, so you hire someone for the job. Then you find an overseas company to manufacture the clothes.

You rush to get it all done, your enthusiasm still sky high, and it's finally ready to launch. But then you realize you've gone way over your budget without noticing until now. Upon investigation, you've found that the marketing manager has received poor reviews for subpar work despite charging an excessive fee. You've also noticed that other qualified professionals are available at a lower cost. Clearly, you made a mistake hiring them.

The clothing from the company you outsourced your production to has just arrived, but it's of very poor quality—another disappointment. Your enthusiasm led you to neglect researching how to save money and to verify the authenticity of the businesses you hired to create your product. These are steps a competent (and experienced) entrepreneur would have taken. As a result, the quality of the clothes falls short of your standards, causing a delay.

You promised customers the launch would be a big event, but now you have to cancel it, leaving people questioning your professionalism.

Thanks to your naïvety, blind optimism has actually put you a step back. You placed too much trust in companies that weren't worthy because you didn't check their credibility. You were only focused on getting everything done straight away.

Be mindful of your enthusiasm; you wouldn't want it to stain your reputation.

Sustainable enthusiasm

Creating sustainable enthusiasm with energy that lasts may sound challenging to some, but it's not as hard as people think. Everyone can achieve it. By applying the following strategies, you will be able to maintain enthusiasm for your passion project until you finish it.

Pace yourself

The first way to avoid burnout is to pace yourself. If you work to the point of exhaustion, you're not being efficient. What's more, it will only kill your enthusiasm for the project, and then you'll never finish it. You want to build sustainable energy that lasts for the length of the project. There is nothing wrong with pacing yourself each step of the way. Some parts may take less time than others.

Keep your energy balanced

Balanced energy sustains momentum. When you start asking yourself questions like: "Is this really worth it? I'm so tired, and I really want to give up," you know you're burning out. This can leave you feeling hopeless and stop you from pursuing your dreams.

Be strategic

You shouldn't need to give up. The project isn't the problem. You are! You're not being strategic in how you carry out the tasks. The tasks can be done, but it's up to you to sustain the energy so you don't burn out.

Focus on one task

If you have an important task with a deadline, but you're also doing other small tasks simultaneously because of your unrealistic expectations, you won't be able to sustain your drive. Sometimes we need to focus on one important task at a time, before going back to the less important ones.

Ease up on the pressure

When you place too much emphasis on efficiency, the project will start to feel insurmountable. You're putting too much pressure on yourself, especially if you don't have a team to back you up.

So, take it step by step, don't try to be too efficient, maintain a healthy balance of enthusiasm and realism, and complete one major task at a time. Let it all fall into place so you can elevate the plan by delegating tasks you can’t handle. You will get busy quickly, so be mindful of how you approach the project from the outset.

Consistent effort trumps emotional highs. Getting overexcited is normal. Just don't let it cloud your judgment. We all feel sensations that seem uncontrollable, but try to come back down from that high to a level of enthusiasm that is sustainable.

Energy that lasts is the kind that pushes us forward each step of the way. It's only after the fact that we realize how quickly we have achieved our dreams by approaching them strategically.

Part V

Your Next Chapter

Monk Mode: A 30-Day Human Reset System

Introduction: What Monk Mode Is

Monk Mode is a 30-day reset for males and females who feel distracted, mentally cluttered, and disconnected from their purpose.

Modern life constantly pulls your attention outward—notifications, temptations, opinions, noise. Over time, this fractures focus, weakens discipline, and dulls self-awareness. Monk Mode removes that noise and brings you back to yourself.

This is not an escape from responsibility. You still work, train, think, and show up. The difference is how you do it—with clarity, intention, and control.

The goal is simple: to realign you with your higher self by rebuilding discipline in the mind, body, and spirit.

Through structured habits, reduced stimulation, and intentional solitude, destructive patterns begin to weaken. Many of these patterns are inherited, learned, or reinforced unconsciously over time. They don't disappear overnight. They break through consistency, patience, and honest effort.

This is not a retreat. You do this at home, in real life. That's what makes it powerful.

You will choose:

- 5 non-negotiable daily practices
- 3 flexible daily practices (your choice on swapping each day)
- 1 weekly practice.

These choices are yours—but honesty is required. Choose what you need, not what feels easy. The system works as long as you do.

Monk Mode strengthens self-control, sharpens awareness of temptation, and retrains the nervous system away from anxiety, fear, and self-doubt, and toward calm focus and internal stability.

Once learned, this becomes a tool you can return to any time.

Why these disciplines matter

Dopamine balance

Most people are overstimulated and underfulfilled.

Modern habits rely on instant dopamine—pornography, substances, junk food, endless scrolling, quick pleasure. These provide short-lived relief but leave the mind restless, dull, and dependent.

Monk Mode replaces artificial highs with earned dopamine—the kind that comes from effort, restraint, and completion.

Examples include:

- training the body
- cold exposure
- focused work
- clean nutrition
- discipline on the hard days

When dopamine is earned rather than consumed, motivation stabilizes. Life feels less chaotic. Focus returns. Boredom fades.

This balance is foundational to clarity and self-control.

Focus

Attention is your most valuable resource—and it's under constant attack.

Fast-paced environments, constant notifications, and endless information fragment your ability to concentrate. This leaves you mentally drained, even when you're busy.

Monk Mode reduces external noise so you can reclaim focus and direct energy toward what actually matters:

- ▹ goals
- ▹ work
- ▹ health
- ▹ family.

With fewer distractions, intuition sharpens. You stop reacting and start choosing.

Focus isn't about doing more.

It's about doing what matters — fully.

Discipline

Motivation is unreliable. Discipline is not.

There will be days you feel driven. There will be many days you don't. Monk Mode is built for the second category.

Discipline is formed when you act despite resistance, not when things feel easy.

This system trains you to:

- ▹ follow through on commitments
- ▹ stay consistent during low-energy days
- ▹ choose long-term growth over short-term comfort.

Most progress happens on the days you don't feel like showing up. Monk Mode conditions you for those days—because they are most of life.

Mental and spiritual clarity

Clarity comes from stillness.

Constant stimulation prevents deep thought and emotional processing. Without space, the mind never settles.

Monk Mode intentionally includes solitude—not isolation, but intentional time alone.

Through walks, reflection, prayer, or mindfulness, you learn to observe your thoughts instead of being controlled by them. You reconnect with values, direction, and internal peace.

This clarity carries into decisions, relationships, and work.

Why a reset works

A reset works because it interrupts destructive momentum.

Patterns weaken when stimulation is removed. Awareness grows when silence is introduced. Discipline strengthens when comfort is reduced.

Thirty days is enough to:

- ▷ break automatic behaviors
- ▷ rewire daily habits
- ▷ restore mental balance
- ▷ prove to yourself that you are capable of control.

Monk Mode doesn't fix your life. It gives you the conditions to rebuild it.

The rules of Monk Mode

Monk Mode works by removing what weakens you and reinforcing what strengthens you.

These rules are not punishments. They are boundaries—and boundaries create freedom.

For 30 days, you commit fully. No half-effort. No loopholes.

The practices

You choose your practices from the list below. Not all are required — consistency is.

There is a list of 20.

You won't be able to do all 20 every day; that's overbearing. Choose the ones that you struggle with and need help to conquer.

- Semen retention (males)
- No drugs, alcohol, or partying
- No social media or doom scrolling
- Training or gym (minimum 5x per week)
- 10,000 steps daily
- Cold showers
- 8 hours sleep
- 15–25 minutes sunlight
- Clean eating, no sugary drinks (water only), and one planned cheat meal per week
- Intermittent fasting (optional)
- 3L of water daily
- Meditation/ mindfulness/ deep prayer
- Solitude & reflection, minimum 15 minutes daily with no distractions
- Journaling
- Daily gratitude list (write 3 things you are grateful for)
- Write 3 daily goals by hand
- Skin care: body scrub (every 3rd day), body wash (daily), body and face cream (daily)
- Dental care: floss, tongue scraper, brush teeth (twice a day for each), mouthwash (once a day)
- One intentional good deed per week

The 30-day structure

Each day includes:

- Core 5 (non-negotiables) - chosen based on your weakest areas and completed daily
- Selectable 3 - flexible practices chosen daily based on need
- Weekly ritual - one added discipline, once a week

Choose honestly. This system only works with integrity.

Signs you're improving

Look for the following signs of improvement:

- calmer mind
- reduced emotional reactivity
- increased focus and energy
- stronger self-control
- less craving for stimulation
- greater self-respect

Your discipline becomes your identity.

Integration: Life after Monk Mode

Monk Mode is a reset, not an escape.

After 30 days:

- reintroduce stimulation slowly
- keep core disciplines
- maintain boundaries

You now know what clarity feels like. Return to Monk Mode any time alignment is lost.

Final word

Monk Mode doesn't add anything to you.

It removes what weakens you.

When distractions fade and discipline sharpens, what remains is clarity, strength, and direction. This is not the end. This is the standard.

The End

"You have power over the mind—not outside events. Realize this, and you will find strength."

— Marcus Aurelius, Meditations

The time has come to begin your own journey as a free thinker.

Living a life opposed to many social norms can be a difficult one, especially in the beginning. But once your breakthrough happens, you will find the peace and freedom everyone seeks. You will be exactly who you want to be, the person life has chosen you to become.

Most people never have this breakthrough. They remain trapped by a limiting mindset they failed to cultivate into an extraordinary one. And they failed to wake up to themselves and get their lives together.

Don't be like most people.

This is the quiet revolution no one else sees. You're making the decision to pursue your plan to become a free thinker with your own values, beliefs, way of thinking, and desired lifestyle. You'll achieve all of this through the quiet battle of overcoming trauma, suffering, and pain—accepting your past life without letting it define who you are in the present moment or who you'll become in the future.

This, right now, is all we have.

It's all that matters.

To have your revolution, you must be willing to accept who you are. You need to acknowledge both the good and evil within so you can see your graces and walk toward the lighter side of life. Be in harmony with yourself and the world that surrounds you. The chaos around you means nothing if you stay true to yourself. No one will see this awakening because it's your vision to become a better person who thinks for themselves. The vision is yours. Do your best to fulfill it, because no one else will do it for you.

In this world, an individual must rely on themselves. It's one of the most critical ways to develop your power. Remain quiet in the process until you're ready to showcase who you are, what you've become, and how you will leave your mark on this planet with the limited time you have.

Everyone is gifted in unique ways, but most people never use their gifts. That's why self-examination is so important—you must sincerely understand what your gift is and how you can use it for the greater good. Some excel at critical and logical thinking, while others are more intuitive and trust their gut. Humans all have different talents, but the patterns remain the same: exercise your advantages to get to the finish line. This is the success you worked hard for.

It doesn't matter where you excel more. What matters is using it to grow every day.

Everyone thinks logically, critically, intuitively, practically, reflectively, independently, skeptically, and creatively. Use all these modes of thinking to your advantage when faced with different experiences, arguments, and situations. Even small experiences can teach you some of your biggest lessons, but they may have escaped your notice. That's why we self-reflect—to look back on what we've missed, connect all the dots, and see how every moment makes sense by shaping us into the person we are now.

Every day, be grateful to wake up. Appreciate every moment. Consistently take steps forward in your growth. Everyone is blessed to have the opportunity to be part of their very own journey of life. Some people have it way tougher than others. Those fortunate enough to be in a blessed position should exercise their free thinking to heal the world.

Keep using all types of thinking. They all come together like instruments in a symphony, where, with the right flow, the composition sounds like a masterpiece. Your mind needs the right flow as a free thinker to elevate with every lesson and opportunity life provides.

It can be a struggle to keep everything in harmony. That's why most people fail to have a full quality of life. The truth is, life is difficult for everyone, no matter the circumstances. None of us will get this perfect, and that's the beauty of it—continually getting it wrong, then eventually getting it right. Moving on to something new, getting that wrong, and learning to get it right. There are no limits to learning. All geniuses get answers wrong. They just have the courage to work with humility and try again, rather than listening to their ego and giving up.

It all starts with the mindset. The principles in this book will guide you to wake up from the reality you once saw into a new one that provides a life of consistent growth.

The mind can be your biggest enemy or your best friend. It's the tool for creating and fixing whatever cards life has dealt you. Everyone constantly battles with their own mind—even the most peaceful people. Learn to control your mind so you can find balance between your light and dark sides. The dark will always be there—it's human nature, but it doesn't have to ruin your life. Exercise your free thinking to develop peace through better habits, especially during times of struggle.

The ups and downs will remain. It's a choice how you choose to respond to situations in your life. In the good times, we can be overexcited, but that doesn't last forever. In hard times, we can be miserable, anxious, and depressed, which also doesn't last forever. It's all about learning how to deal with the highs and lows so you can overcome every experience. The mind should not be mistreated—it should be embraced to continue the journey, closing each chapter to pursue a more positive opportunity.

Having a controlled mind makes you dangerous, but in a humble way. Not for selfish and evil reasons. People will never understand you because you're so unique. They try, but will never get the satisfaction if they're not deserving to know the real you. These are the people who show jealousy, ill intentions, and doubt. I'm not saying you should be hateful toward them. Be kind to them as they're struggling with their own identity. They have no idea who you are, but they see a light in you that freaks them out. That's why everyone takes shots at accomplished individuals—innovative entrepreneurs or creative artists who are super successful. It's the price of being dangerous. The world will come at you and try to tear you down.

You know who you are. Remain grounded and unbreakable. Keep fighting to be the best version of yourself.

Never lose your humble mentality because the world has gotten into your head. This life remains a journey, never a destination. No one knows where they'll end up in a decade. Embrace the unknown, but never look too far forward into it because it doesn't exist. There's nothing there for us. We can have a plan that directs us to where we'd like to end up; everyone needs direction, of course. But in reality, all we have is today, so focus on the task you need to get done right now, step by step, so you can keep the process going until, finally, when the day comes, your goal is achieved.

Stop rushing. Stop getting too far forward in your head. Pace yourself. There is no race with humanity. Your goal will be achieved if you believe. Just know there's a journey involved before you get to the destination. The journey is the most important part, testing you to see if you can break free from the limitations of your past self. Once you do, breakthroughs in mindset keep coming.

Now go out there and make a difference in the world as an extraordinary free thinker.

Channel these impressive talents. This won't only change your life, but also the lives of those around you. You may even inspire people you don't know. It's a blessing to serve humanity by cultivating a productive mindset that turns you into a person with virtuous qualities you can spread to others.

It's amazing how a person can transform their life from darkness to glory in a small period of time. The miracles are there, and they happen every day. It's time to open your eyes and see the beauty of it all. Once you see it, you become the difference in others' lives.

That's the journey of a free thinker.

Welcome to the revolution.

www.ingramcontent.com/pod-product-compliance
Lightning Source LLC
LaVergne TN
LVHW010053110826
845155LV00028B/314